DO YOUR OWN PUBLICITY

Terry Prone

POOLBEG

Acknowledgements

People who read and amended sections of this book and who allowed me to exploit their insight and experience include David Curtin, Public Relations Manager, National Lottery, Mary Murphy, Director Public Relations, Carr Communications and Donal Cronin, Senior Account Executive, Carr Communications.

My thanks also to Fionnuala O'Kelly, whose briefing to local PROs says a lot of what's here, only more briefly, and to Sinead Gorby, who lent me source material and trusted me to give it back.

Frank Drumm, Managing Director of Securicor, told me the story on pages 90 to 91 and provided the picture. Tom Hudson, Chief Executive of the Irish Cancer Society, generously let me tell the success story of Daffodil Day.

If Robert Spencer had not invited me to address a meeting of the "Business Development Programme Association," the book would never have been started and without Mary Boyle and Gerard Kenny, it would never have been finished.

Jo O'Donoghue is an editor who manages to be clear, demanding and encouraging all at once—it's a joy to work for her.

For Anton Savage

A Very Special Friend

Contents

1

Why You Need Publicity —and This Book

THE possibility of reading your name in a newspaper or hearing your voice on radio makes you break out in hives. You have lived happily up to now without people stopping you in the street and asking for your autograph and you don't feel under pressure to get an unlisted telephone number. You don't have an overwhelming need to be a household name or to have your own face beaming down at you from roadside posters. But you figure that publicity has its uses. Its costs. Its threats.

You're right.

This book is geared to helping you minimise the costs and the threats and to making the best use of publicity. If you really need it.

But why might you need it?

You may need publicity if you are in any one of the following situations:

- You're a singer, talented enough to make it, but scared of becoming yet another example of the sad near-successes immortalised in the song "Rock and Roll I Gave You All the Best Years of My Life."
- You're an actor nobody has yet heard of, caught in the vicious circle of obscurity: "Come back to us when you have a few worthwhile credits to your name."
- You're a TV or radio performer who wants to go places, but who never seems to get mentioned in the right columns.
- You're a would-be politician.
- You're part of a pressure group, trying to change the law or public attitudes on something which affects a specific group or the wider public. A pressure group can be made up of people wanting better treatment for the elderly, it can be

composed of environmentalists or anti-abortionists or gay rights activists.

- You're part of a non-profit or voluntary group that needs to be better known so that its fundraising will be more fruitful or its membership bigger.
- You're part of a social or athletic group and want to introduce a pastime to larger numbers of the public than have engaged in it up to now.
- You own or run a business. Publicity for the business, its services or its products would be helpful to your bottom line.

If you are in any of these positions, this book is written for you, to show you how to get the right publicity in the right places, and—whenever possible—how to get that publicity without paying for it.

There are lots of other possibilities. Including the desire to be famous just for the hell of it. Nobody ever admits to this, just as nobody ever admits to lacking a sense of humour or being a poor driver, but there are a lot of people who would dearly love to be just a little bit famous and have their friends mention to them what the newspaper said about them last week.

Publicity rarely happens by accident. Somebody usually seeds the clouds. Somebody always has. It may only be in recent years that we have had highly paid publicity consultants, PR people and image "handlers" springing up right and left, but history is peopled by great men who not only achieved deeds which focused the minds of their contemporaries, but who frequently timed those deeds in order to get the maximum contemporary, retrospective and mythical coverage. (I say great *men* advisedly. In the past, behind every great man was a great woman, and that's not a great position to be in if you plan a little personal image-building. If the public can't see you and don't learn your name, you end up, if you're lucky, with a grateful mate and zilch public persona.)

Sometimes the seeded clouds continue to rain publicity long after the publicity is useful. Even now, in the early nineties, it's difficult to get away from the faces of Marilyn Monroe and Jacqueline Kennedy, even though one is dead for almost three decades and the other has avoided publicity so relentlessly that she has even taken one street photographer—a "paparazzo" named Ron Galella—to court in order to ensure that he stays more than fifty feet away from her.

Not only do the seeded clouds continue to drizzle, in some cases, long after the initial burst of publicity, but sometimes, what comes down is acid rain. Early in her career, feminist Gloria Steinem joined one of Hefner's Bunny Clubs as a Bunny Girl, floppy ears, scut attached to her bottom, high heels and all, in order to glean the material needed for a magazine exposé of this supposedly glamour job. She got a good story, but *Playboy*, as part of their normal personnel process, got a good picture of Steinem in bunny clothing, which they ran repeatedly in later years as she chipped away at sexploitation. It became *Playboy*'s long-running revenge.

Arguably the saddest example of continuing unsought acid publicity rain happened to the man who intervened when a woman drew a gun on then President Ford in San Francisco in 1975. Oliver Sipple, a thirty-three-year-old passerby, deflected the gun and saved the President's life. He was an instant hero, and the newspapers, radio and television started to dig to find interesting details about his private life.

Sipple not only didn't encourage the publicity, he actively asked media people to ignore him, which inevitably whetted the collective appetite even more. One newspaper suggested that gay men would be very proud of Sipple. Why? Because he had been involved in gay causes. Was he gay? He refused to say.

"My sexual orientation has nothing at all to do with saving the President's life," he said, truthfully.

That didn't stop a newspaper in his home town going to his mother and telling *her* he was gay. She was so shocked that she refused to speak to him for the rest of her life, and on her death, his father refused to have him at the funeral. Sipple became a lonely heavy-drinking man who died a solitary death in 1989.

Publicity has its positive side and its negative side, and before you launch into an attempt to make yourself or your cause or your company famous, you need to think about both.

But let's take a quick look at the list of people who, I suggested, might need publicity. Singers and actors? Yes, you nod. Of course. People get booked to do concerts because they're famous, and they get famous because they've appeared in a hit show or had a hit song, and publicity can help them through the early stages to reach that point.

But broadcasters? Local politicians? People running charities?

All of these people can profit from publicity. Let me give you a few anonymous case histories.

Case History # 1:

The Broadcaster

He was everybody's best pal in the station. If you were stuck for a link, he'd bang out forty-five seconds of pure magic on his little portable typewriter. If you needed to get the right pronunciation for a placename, he would have it. If you needed the name of the guy who played bass guitar on an obscure recording, he knew it. He was the guy you could call on when the early morning DJ was too hungover to answer his phone. The guy who never made a fuss about working a public holiday. He was a *given*. An assumption. And he was fed up with it, he told me one day, when he asked me to have coffee with him. "You going to turn nasty?" I asked him, trying to imagine it.

"No, but I want to turn famous," he said, actually gritting his teeth to get the words out.

This surprised me even more. After all, he was on the radio five evenings a week, wasn't he?

"That's not famous," he said bluntly. "I'm on in the evening because I'm *acceptable*. If I were famous and popular I'd be on during the daytime. Now, the station is starting a second radio network, and I want to be upfronted when it goes on the air."

In order to do that, he needed, he believed, the referred credibility of visibility, as opposed to audible fame, and he wanted my help. Together we examined his biography, identified odd streaks of knowledge only he had, plus access to world-famous figures only he had. Out of that came guest appearances on a series of TV shows, and, in due course, a higher profile position on radio. Most of the publicity he won for himself, simply by sitting down beside people in the broadcasting station canteen and making a suggestion to a producer or presenter; except that this time the suggestion in some way involved their use of his talents. He no longer wanted to be an anonymous human archive and general boy scout. What was so successful about it was that nobody noticed that there was a plan behind it. As people congratulated the broadcaster, they told him they were delighted that at long last, *other* people were finally learning to appreciate his value.

Case History # 2: The Politician

"I doubt very much if you can help me," he said as he poured me tea.

This got the conversation off to a fairly hairy start. I wanted coffee, for one thing. For another, to have someone make an appointment and then tell you that your services are probably unhelpful tends to be a demotivating introduction. I ingested tannin and waited.

"You've never heard of me," he went on accusingly.

I admitted it.

"I'm 26," he said. (He looked older.) "And I want to be in government. Right now, I haven't even been elected to anything but my local Credit Union and football club, but that's what I want to do and I figure I can't do it without being famous because my father was never in politics." It took me a little while to work out that since his father had never been in politics, this meant that he could not "inherit" a parliamentary seat, and (to mix a metaphor or two) was in a greenfield situation. There was a political party to which he had a leaning, but he had yet to join it.

"You want to be famous before you do anything else?"

"Well, I'm getting on with other things, but if I haven't a famous name, I've got to create one, right?"

I nodded.

"So how much?"

I looked blankly at him. "How much *what*?"

"How much money will it cost for you to PR me?"

I told him it was a little like the old story of the

countryman, asked for directions as to how to get to a particular town. After a moment's thought, the countryman said that if he was going to that town, he wouldn't start from where he was. Similarly, I told my new acquaintance, money was the least of his worries. He was going to have to work out, first of all, what he stood for, what he cared about, how to align his concerns with those of voters, how to make these concerns interesting to a media audience, how to structure his life and his thinking to make the most, in the long-term, of publicity.

"In the long term?" he repeated, worriedly.

"Yeah," I said. "What did you think, that you'd get famous for a month and then forget it?"

Eventually, we parted, and I forgot about him. Six months later, he surfaced again, this time complete with documentation about his plans, his beliefs and his team. I sat down with him (over coffee this time) and began to shape a publicity programme for him.

"Why are you *telling* me these things," he suddenly said, irritated. "I'm prepared to pay you to do them for me."

I had to explain to him that it is not a good idea for a novice politician to arrive on the national scene covered in handlers.

He was going to have to create a number of relationships. he was going to have to look eager and professional, but not processed and veneered. He was going to have to knock on a good few doors himself, and create the stories to deliver when the doors opened. None of this appealed to him. He had assumed that a PR retainer to a consultant would take away all of that unpleasant directness and hard sell. But he eventually faced up to it and did it. Today, he has a perfect political profile in his middle years. He is functionally famous and has never lost the capacity to generate a headline when the image slips a bit. Not so long ago, he told me that he still feels guilty that his image was based on what I had told him, but he'd never paid for it.

"You should write a book," he said. "And tell people how my image was created."

Small pause.

"But you wouldn't give my name, sure you wouldn't?"

Case History # 3:

Pressure Groups Against Media

We move across the Atlantic for this one, because although there have been many protests about the limitations on broadcasting material involving the IRA in both Britain and Ireland, pressure groups have made less impact on this side of the water when it comes to influencing the way media—in particular television—handle particular groups.

At any given time, you can be sure that someone somewhere is enraged about a recent or up-coming TV programme's treatment of women, older people, blacks, gays or children. Occasionally that rage is managed and funded so that notice is taken of it. One example was when the TV series *Maude* decided to have its central character have an abortion. The Catholic Church in the United States campaigned with carefully-aimed vigour, causing most sponsors to pull their advertising, and prompting forty stations across the US to drop the controversial episodes.

The Catholic Church is a large and unified entity. Theoretically, those who are passionately against the existence and use of nuclear weapons are a more dispersed pressure group. Nevertheless, in 1983, they saw their chance to climb on a bandwagon and spark a lot of public debate relatively cheaply. The bandwagon was provided by the planned showing of the TV programme *The Day After*, which was a three-hour movie illustrating the aftermath of nuclear war. The film became a rallying point for nuclear freeze advocates. To promote their cause, they orchestrated a national campaign around *The Day After*, involving more than 1,000 grassroot organisations—and publicising the fact that so many organisations were involved. They set up a free telephone answering service for several days to answer questions arising from the movie, and got publicity for that, too. To attract free press coverage, they held candlelight vigils, political rallies and marches.

Inevitably, the right-wingers struck back, with the leader of the Moral Majority calling the anti-nuclear activists a threat to America's national security. The network broadcasting the programme decided it couldn't ignore all of this reaction. So, whether to assuage the activists or simply to capitalise on the well-articulated passions, ABC followed the showing of the movie with a discussion which featured famous upholders of the "we gotta have our A-bomb" line against those who wanted arms control.

Who won this battle is not clear. Why it deserves attention is that, for the outlay of relatively little hard cash, a group turned a three hour movie into the "most politicised entertainment programme ever seen on TV."

Case History # 4:
Publicity for Fundraising

There will be lots of examples, later in this book, of non-profit organisations ranging from Greenpeace to the Irish Cancer Society. But for our case history, let's plug in to a colleague of mine who was asked to lunch by a man he hadn't seen in ten years. When they both sat down to eat, the friend awkwardly got to the point. He did a little fundraising for the college they had both attended in their teens. Would my pal Derek now contribute to the fundraising effort?

How much did he want, Derek asked. The friend gazed at him, dumb with misery.

Seriously, Derek said. How much did the man want from Derek's back pocket? The man dithered and said anything Derek fancied. £25? £50?

When Derek pushed his soup plate away and sighed, the man panicked and said that even a tenner would help.

No, Derek told him, he would not contribute. Not money, anyway, because he had a series of personal pet charities and he gave all spare money to them. But he suggested the man not waste the lunch he was buying.

"What are you asking money *for*?"

"Well, the college," the man said.

"Nothing special about the college, even though I went there," Derek said. "What *within* the college do you want to do things with?"

After a long time, it emerged that an old roof of particularly distinctive craftsmanship had been severely damaged by a falling tree, and would be costly to repair, that a particular line of scientific research was currently operating within a cramped laboratory, and that the college choir, which was beginning to win international awards, needed a new rehearsal room with improved acoustics. Derek drew up a two-page plan to make all of these issues saleable to media at home and overseas, and a related two-page plan to fundraise, using the publicity as a starting-block.

He also suggested to the man that overseas fundraising was a necessity, that the amounts then being sought should be multiplied by ten, a hundred or a thousand, and that the entire operation should be professionalised. Within a year, the College had netted one million pounds, which was at least seven hundred and fifty thousand pounds more than they had originally planned to make. In reporting this to Derek, and in asking him (for money, this time) to advise on further publicity/fundraising the old college pal announced that the most surprising thing about the whole year was the rise in morale within the college.

"Somehow, seeing the College reported on in overseas, fairly prestigious magazines, made everybody feel they were part of something worthwhile. I mean, we all *knew* we were part of something worthwhile," he added hastily.

"Yeah, but it helps to have a little outside confirmation," Derek smiled. "Especially when they put it in cold print. When it goes into print, not only can you read it again and again, but you can also buy up a few thousand of the magazine and circulate it to the specific target publics. Best introduction in the world. "Never mind the boasts we'd like to make about us, let's just show you what the London *Times* or *Time* Magazine have said about us..."

Case History # 5:

Sporting Groups

Not so long ago, a parachuting group decided that they wanted to let people know about parachuting as a sport. So they contacted a number of journalists and broadcasters and invited them to make a jump. One TV producer took a jump and became an instant parachute addict, finding wonderful ways to include parachuting in all sorts of programmes he was making. So enthusiastic did he get that he infected a newscaster, who decided to emulate his now experienced friend. The newscaster made his initial jump and had a complex and damaging landing, which effectively pulped his leg, and left him a) with a limp, and b) with no great enthusiasm for parachuting. The moral here would seem to be "when you're getting coverage, don't push your luck!"

Case History # 6:

How Small Business Created a Publicity Book

They didn't look like small business people. They didn't look like *small* anything. They looked like success stories—which they were.

Some of them had taken over ailing family businesses and cured what ailed them, which sometimes included members of the family.

Some of them had been involved in management

buyouts which had turned the fortunes of their companies right around.

Some of them had started their own businesses with a bright idea, a little help from a friendly bank manager, and an awful lot of personal blood, tears and sweat.

Now, they had decided to examine what Public Relations could do for them, and they had invited me along to talk to them.

- About Corporate Communications Strategy. (Thoughtful nods).
- About PR support for their marketing drives. (Notes taken on Filofax pages.)
- About publicity which did the company bottom line good, as opposed to making the Chief Executive feel warm and glowy. (They all indicated that they weren't that kind of Chief Executive.)
- About PR costs. Average retainers currently obtaining.

At this point, sickness as of afflicted parrot broke out on all sides. I gave the figures, and silence fell so heavily you felt you should dodge.

"I don't know about the rest of you," one of the entrepreneurs said. "But I couldn't afford half of that in any year."

A supportive murmur rose from the group. None of them could envisage finding an average PR retainer from their annual turnover.

"What if we went to a PR company and said "Look, we can only pay you £5,000 a year, and we want really good service, but if you play your cards right, we'll get bigger and you'll do well out of it, too?"

All faces turned hopefully to me as this suggestion

was articulated.

"It's always worth a try," I agreed. "Particularly with a reasonably new PR company that's hungry for business. But any of the larger firms will either give you a blunt refusal, or they will agree and then, of necessity, shunt you to the most junior executive or keep postponing your problems while they deal with the problems of their big payers."

Another silence whomped into place.

"Could any of us do our own publicity?" a woman asked.

"You have already *done* your own publicity," a man across the table from her responded.

"No, I haven't. Sure, there have been stories on me in the papers, but they just happened. I didn't make them happen. And they weren't the kind of stories that were any use to my company, anyway. But what I'm thinking now is, maybe I could do my own publicity, get my own coverage."

"Wouldn't work. No journalist is going to talk to you unless you're a proper PR person."

The statement came from one of the business people present, the rest of whom instantly looked to me for confirmation.

"Curiously," I said, "The reverse is sometimes true. Journalists who hate PR people have no problems at all being contacted by a businessman or woman who thinks they've got a story. You must remember that there are journalists who regard PR as a parasitic and unnecessary trade, who dump PR material almost by reflex, and who feel warmer about bubonic plague than about taking phone calls from PR Account Executives."

Knowing that my company is in the PR business, the group looked hurt on my behalf.

"OK, let's say we decided to do it ourselves—do our

own publicity, get our own coverage, handle our own PR, is there a book that would help us organise it?"

The Parkers all poised in unison over the little note-taking pages, and I searched for words of wisdom. They were thin on the ground and everywhere else.

"There *should* be a book," I agreed weakly. "But to my knowledge there isn't one."

A brisk suggestion came from them that I should write it.

So here it is. And I hope it creates lots of case histories showing small businesses winning the publicity they deserve and using it well.

2

Why You Haven't Had Publicity up to Now

Before you get down to planning an effective PR programme for yourself, your company or your organisation, let's address some of the justifications you may be using to cover the fact that you haven't made it onto the front pages or into radio and TV programmes up to now.

"They're Only Interested in Bad News"

So are most people. How often do you enter your household and say "Wait till I tell you, folks. Today I had a really pleasant day. The Boss was nice to me. The coffee out of the machine was every bit as good as usual and the climate was acceptable for this time of the year"?

If you arrive home and announce that the toll bridge got stuck in the air for twenty minutes with a van full of screaming toddlers in it, that your Boss has run away with his own or someone else's secretary, or that someone infected your computer with a pornographic videogame virus, *then* you're likely to get a bit of attention.

But not just because what you have to offer is bad news. (You may quite enjoy the porno video game and the errant Boss, at least in the short term, is going to be a happy camper with the equally errant secretary). What makes you more interesting, in this instance, is that you are telling something which is *new* or *different* or *unexpected* or *vivid*.

If you want publicity for yourself, your product, your organisation or your company, then rid yourself, fast, of the notion that what is routine, as long as it is worthy, should get headlines. What is routine, *ipso facto*, does not deserve headlines, and if it is worthy as well as routine, it will shrivel the soul of any editor or producer. Ask any kid who is made to eat porridge every day of its life. Being told that it's good for them makes it taste worse, not better.

The myth that media people are only interested in bad news has been around a long time. Media people are interested in *news*, full stop.

"They're All Pinkos and They Don't Want to Know Anybody Else"

Or they're all right wing conservatives with fascist tendencies.

At any given time, there is a lively conspiracy theory surrounding radio stations and newspapers, which holds that their thinking is dominated by one particular political (or religious) philosophy.

This theory sees all of the sub-editors at the particular station or paper working overtime to slide subtle comments into coverage which reflect well on "their side," and unsubtle negatives which cast aspersions on "our side."

This theory goes further. It listens to tones and inflections and looks at expression:

- "Did you *hear* the way he asked that question?"
- "Did you see the raised eyebrow on her when she was winding up that discussion?"

I once had a client, in the grip of such a conspiracy theory, who wanted to sue a newspaper which had described him as a seminal influence on something or other. Try as I might, I could not detach him from the conviction that the use of the word "seminal" meant the comment was slander, dirt and not the thing he would want his mother to read about him in a daily newspaper.

Many journalists and broadcasters have strong political feelings. They also have arms, legs and sometimes a smattering of false teeth, but we don't usually hold these attributes against them. In fact, we don't usually give them a second thought. Nor should we waste our own good time speculating or becoming paranoid about the possible political or religious affiliations of the people who may write about us.

Most journalists are fair. Most journalists have a strong ethical sense. Those who are known to subscribe to a particular code tend to make an extra effort in order to be seen not to discriminate against opposing views.

"If You Try Ringing Them Up, They're Rude"

Let's say there is a journalist in a newsroom, surrounded by perhaps thirty other journalists, all of them pounding on keyboards, yelling into telephones or telling each other jokes in corners.

This journalist is working for a newspaper which is coming under pressure as its circulation figures wane just a little. A new Features Editor has been brought in to shake things up a little, and the word is that she's a tough egg. Our journalist hasn't yet been summoned to The Presence, so he's writing away in ignorance, trying to guess at what she likes so that he won't start behind the eight ball. But because he may never find the eight ball, he's also doing little nixer jobs for other departments in the newspaper, for the local radio station and for a magazine, just so he will have somewhere to go if push comes to shove.

At his desk, he works in an urgent crouch, pursued by deadlines and dogged by fear that the new Features Editor will arrive silently behind him and read, on his VDU, the quiz on How To Judge Your Sex Appeal that he's busily crafting for a new woman's mag.

The phone he shares with the writer next door has been tweeting at him for some time, and, resigning himself to the fact that nobody but him is going to pick it up and deal with it, he lifts the receiver.

"Is that Jason Throckmorton?" the voice at the other end asks.

The journalist sinks more wearily into his chair. Jason Throckmorton is a mythical figure, created by a former editor to cover a gossip column so that the writing of said column could be shared by several journalists, rather than handed over, dripping as it was in freebie champagne and promotional trips to exotic places, to one single writer. Our weary journalist has a small piece of the Jason Throckmorton action, but he rarely admits it.

"OK, what is it you want?"

It's not an admission, but in his view, it's enough to be going on with.

"I want to speak to Jason Throckmorton."

"He's not here at the moment, can I take a message for—"

"When will Jason be there?"

"Look, we all work together here, would you like to tell me what you're ringing about?"

"Well, I suppose if Jason isn't there. Really what I want to comment about is the way you just put the same pictures in all the time and the same people. Not that I want to complain, but I have this very interesting business and nobody has ever done a story on it, and I don't understand why and I'd like you—well, really, I'd like Jason to come out and do a story on it."

"What sort of a business is it?"

"Well, it's quite like the one he's written about in this morning's paper."

"It's unlikely he'd be interested in doing something that's a carbon copy."

"It's not a carbon copy, we were here first, but no journalist ever pays us any attention. It's not what you know, it's *who* you know, isn't it?"

At this point, our journalist is good and cheesed off and has the caller squarely positioned on the disposal chute.

"Look, send Jason a note about it, OK?" he says and cradles the phone.

The caller sends "Jason" a letter which is eighty percent complaint against the nameless hack who answered the phone. The letter ends up on the desk of a quite different journalist who disapproved of the first feature done on this theme, sure as hell is not going to promote a second feature, and who therefore consigns it quickly to the shredder.

"You Have To Be Pals with Them before They'll Cover Your Story"

Not only do you *not* have to be pals with a journalist in order to get him or her to cover your story, your chances may be improved by being an anonymous new face. Journalists who are pals of yours may be self-conscious about giving you a "plug", whereas total strangers may be much more open to your approaches.

Where being pals with journalists can pay off is in

follow-up publicity. You have an interesting story to tell and a journalist writes it up, a photographer takes a series of pictures and you buy six copies of the paper (in six different shops, in case they spot you). Some time later, the same journalist is doing a story about workaholics, and, rifling through his mental files about executives, comes up with your name, puts a telephone call through to you and gets a quote. The few sentences you deliver over the phone get mated to a variant on the first photo which appeared, and there is your follow-up publicity.

One household name of my acquaintance laughs when people compliment her on what they call her "publicity machine."

"My machine is a phone," she smiles. "And a civil answer. When journalists ring up, I try to be helpful. I answer questions, whether they're about clothes or travel or Christmas presents or books or taste in food. They put me in their stories, my profile stays high and everybody assumes I have a publicity machine!"

"You Have To Waste an Awful Lot of Time Making Phone Calls"

Correction. If you're seeking publicity for yourself, your organisation or your company, you will certainly have to *spend* an awful lot of time on it. A public presence is not easily established, nor is it easily maintained. That is why most large companies hand the task over to a consultancy which is geared to do it efficiently and well; the MD of the client company does not have to waste time away from core business chatting up a journalist or FAXing a press release.

It's something worth considering, before you plunge

ahead on manufacturing your own publicity.

It doesn't come for free.

Yes, if you do your own publicity, you save yourself the very considerable retainer you would otherwise pay a PR company. Retainers tend to start around the £10,000 a year mark and work upwards in great quantum leaps, depending on the complexity of the task.

On the other hand, while you may not be spending money, you will almost certainly be spending *time*. Time spent being interrupted and deflected from the essentials of your own job can be very expensive time indeed and should be calculated before you embark on the self-publicist's route.

Within a small company or a charity, it does not always have to be the top man or woman who does the publicity. Someone down the line who has enthusiasm, and a "feel" for what the operation is all about may be a much better choice. Even if you are a one-woman or one-man operation, a pal may be persuaded to do a little part-time contact work on your behalf. This latter option has the added advantage that someone *who is not you* is able to say that you are wonderful with much more conviction than you may muster when pushing yourself.

"You Have To Have a Hard-Sell Personality"

Not so. Journalists are just as put off as the rest of the world by a fast-talking peddler of glib. What you *must* have is the capacity to tell your story clearly, positively, and briefly. If you are too shy to do that, then see above.

"Journalists Have To Be Bribed before They'll Cover Your Product or Company"

Oooh. Shhhh. Tsk, tsk. Let us not have wild sloshes of libel and slander here.

Some journalists get some freebies some of the time. Of that we can all be quite sure. When I was beauty correspondent for a national newspaper, I was constantly up to my armpits in little caskets filled with sweet-smelling gloop for the face, pastel tubes bulging with chemical creams for removing hair or supplying blush, and tiny plastic containers holding eye-shadows of improbable colours. All of these were sent to me ostensibly as items for me to experiment with and report on, ruthlessly and judgementally, to my readers. In fact, they were gifts hoping for a mention.

Tubes of gloop are one thing. Major bribery is another. Most newspapers and radio/TV stations now have at least a theoretical divide between the two. Not all are as honest as a radio producer I once worked for. Her presenter, a household name, happened to mention, on the air, that he had never eaten passion fruit, and wondered what it tasted like. This was apropos of nothing in particular. He was simply filling in time between records.

A smart supermarket chain heard the item, and within an hour, an open cardboard container, holding 24 promising passion fruit, had been delivered to the radio station. The producer looked at them, looked at her staff, all of whom shared the presenter's ignorance of passion fruit and willingness to experiment on same, and sent them back with a pleasant note saying

"Thanks. No thanks. He's paid enough to buy his own."

Some property supplements have had to introduce rules which say that if you take their journalist on a trip to see your development out in Tenerife, more power to you, but he will not be able to write about it. If you want it written about, send in the information and the pictures. In other words, "just the facts, Ma'am."

There are some journalistic areas where the line between a plug and a judgement is awfully fine. Motoring columns stand squarely on that line. Motoring correspondents get taken on trips all over the world by car makers, who are convinced that a journalist cannot do serious justice to their latest MJK 523 Zx#*! unless they see it in action, first on the sands of the Sahara, then on the icy slopes of Everest, and finally on the road at Monte Carlo. Motoring journalists taken on these trips undoubtedly report accurately what they find out about the car, but it is notable that theatre critics (who only get free tickets to a show) are given to more explicit savagery than are the wheel writers.

Whether it's a specialist journalist you're dealing with, or a general reporter, the fact is that they do not have to be bribed, most of them would be appalled by the suggestion that they *could* be bribed, and many of them are put off doing a story by proffered freebies. If it is important, in order to understand the functioning of a gadget, that a journalist gets a free one, fair enough. If it is not important, then tell your story and do not insult the scribe by assuming he or she needs palms crossed with anything.

"I Did Make a Suggestion, but They Turned It Down"

If you're looking for publicity, you will have to come to terms with rejection. The first time someone finds your story uninteresting, you want to crawl away into a hole and cease to be. The second time, you feel a confirmed failure.

The third time, it's down to Dorothy Parker's options.

> *Razors pain you*
> *Rivers are damp;*
> *Acids stain you;*
> *And drugs cause cramp.*
> *Guns aren't lawful,*
> *Nooses give;*
> *Gas smells awful:*
> *You might as well live...*
>
> Dorothy Parker

The capacity to sustain rejection is natural to a minority of people, and developed slowly, in pain and misery, by the rest of us. In publicity-seeking, you have to behave like one of those ashtrays on long stalks with a weight at the bottom: wallop it in one direction and it goes with the blow, bouncing right back up to where it was in the first place.

Remember that when you are trying to interest a journalist or broadcaster, you are a sales rep. You are selling an idea. For every sale you make, there will be five or ten or fifteen sales you lose. Don't cradle the phone after a rejection. Cut off the call you've just made and dial the next one.

"You Can't Control What They End Up Saying"

You're dead right, you can't. They may make mistakes. Or they may take a negative position on the story. That's a risk you have to face up to when you are seeking publicity if you are not rich enough to work your way around it.

There is a classic example of a company which *is* rich enough to work their way around what they saw as repeated misinformation stories about their business in newspapers. This is Mobil, the American oil giant. Large oil corporations were repeatedly on the unpopular side of arguments from the 'sixties onwards, and Mobil, in common with many others, found that even the most assertive, information-filled public relations was not getting their story to the people they wanted to reach.

So they bought their way out of the problem. What they did was purchase sections of "opinion-forming" sections of prestigious newspapers like the *New York Times* to state their corporate view on anything from mass transit systems to the interference of the American Supreme Court in matters commercial, from the screening of the controversial TV programme *Death of a Princess* to the nature of the capitalist system. Mobil's ads got noticed. One particular series of eleven related advertisements discussing energy policy was offered to the interested public in the form of free reprints. 25,000 copies were asked for.

"When you're selling ideas, the results are especially hard to quantify," says Herb Schmertz, Mobil Oil's Vice President for Public Affairs. "But it's clear that through our op-ed ads, we've managed to bring some of our views into the public consciousness."

The only problem with all of that is that if you're reading this book because you want to achieve your own publicity for free, you don't have the cash to think about by-passing journalists and going directly into print with "advertising editorial." So you have to supply information in the clearest possible form, and take the risk that the journalist may say something you would prefer to see unsaid.

"You Would Have To Buy Ads in Their Publications"

As a card-carrying NUJ member, I would love to be able to put a hand on my heart and say Get thee behind me, Slanderer. But you could be right. There are small sniffy pockets of journalism where if you don't buy an ad you don't see your story in print. It happens most often in semi-sporadic, not-too-permanent magazines whose corporate priority is cashflow rather than ethics. It also happens in advertising features, where if you buy an ad, you are likely, surprise, surprise, to turn up in the copy around which all of the ads are displayed.

Buying ads in the hope of linked copy is the road to no town. It demoralises the spender, who feels dirtied by the proceeding, it cheats the public, who ought to be able to believe what it reads in "editorial matter", and it muddies the water for the rest of us poor slobs who are out there trying to win space on the basis of simple newsworthiness, rather than organisational bribes.

The good news is that you can survive without buying positive mentions. My own company, about ten years ago, innocently took a holier than thou stance on this, mainly because we had no money, at the time, to pay for the ads. We figure, looking at the press coverage of the intervening decade, that we lost nothing in serious, credible coverage by refusing to buy the interest of the papers involved.

"You Would Have No Privacy Any More"

It depends on what way you position your story. There are supermarket chains which tell their story in terms of cheapness—and there are supermarket chains which tell their story in the high profile person of one of their key people. That key person, if he (she) figures on radio, TV and newspaper ads, and is the one chosen by the media for comment on price wars and other retailer-related stories, becomes a household name. This can be an enjoyable experience, I'm told. Rather them than me, frankly. The individual who gets out in front of a concept or a business and fronts for it can end up as fast food for public consumption. Heavy on the willing responsiveness, hold the privacy. For a sensitive individual, it can be torture.

“You Couldn’t Be Sure How Valuable a Mention in a Newspaper or an Appearance on TV Really Is”

You know the old saw about advertising? 50% of every advertising budget is totally wasted. The only problem is working out *which* 50%.

The impact of publicity is very difficult to measure. So difficult that I am secretly convinced that one of the main reasons why captains of industry make such an effort to achieve “a prestigious corporate profile” is that they get quiet thrills from reading about themselves in the financial papers, even though a picture of them, jaw outthrust to indicate strength, glasses clasped in hand to indicate thoughtfulness, mineral water within reach to indicate sobriety, may have little or no impact on the corporate bottom line.

There are a lot of businesspeople who are not sure that they exist if they don’t see themselves mentioned in media on a monthly or weekly basis, and if you are one of them, don’t waste your time trying to achieve objective justifications for time spent achieving publicity. We’re all entitled to our little luxuries and, although publicity is as addictive as drink, it does less harm to the liver.

Quite seriously, unpurchased publicity can do enormous good to a business. Readers know the difference between an ad and editorial matter, and they tend to value the latter much more than the former. In other words, whereas an ad may attract their attention, it will also attract their scepticism. They read the copy which suggests that this product will change their lives and is the best ever invented, and they mentally say "Yes, but that's just a claim made by the manufacturer in an ad that manufacturer is paying for."

Editorial material in the same publication may not be quite so visually attractive, but neither does it attract such scepticism. A fearless reporter, whose words have not been bought and paid for by you, but who nonetheless says your product will change everybody's lives and is a major breakthrough, is much more believable. My company, when it was dirt poor in the first five years of its life, made the decision that it could not afford to pay for advertising and therefore must depend, for public profile, on whatever stories journalists crafted about our operation. When it started to make money, it didn't change its stance; we had learned that personnel managers who wanted development training for their executives paid much more attention to the objective reporting of business journalists than they did to even the most attractive advertising.

None of which helps in this scenario: You have achieved a full page feature on your company's operations in one of the Sunday newspaper magazines. The pictures are good. The copy is positive. All names are spelt correctly. But when everybody has stopped being personally pleased, how does management quantify the value of the piece?

The PR rationale for this purpose goes like this. Count the pages covered by the feature. 2½. Find the cost of a full page of full colour advertising in that publication. £20,000? OK. So in strict advertising terms, the coverage has been worth £50,000 to the company. But then, (the PR rationale goes on) because people value the content of editorial pages so much more highly than they value advertising pages, you multiply that by a factor of five. Some people suggest that the factor should be greater than five. One way or the other, your coverage is worth money—and it is money you have not spent.

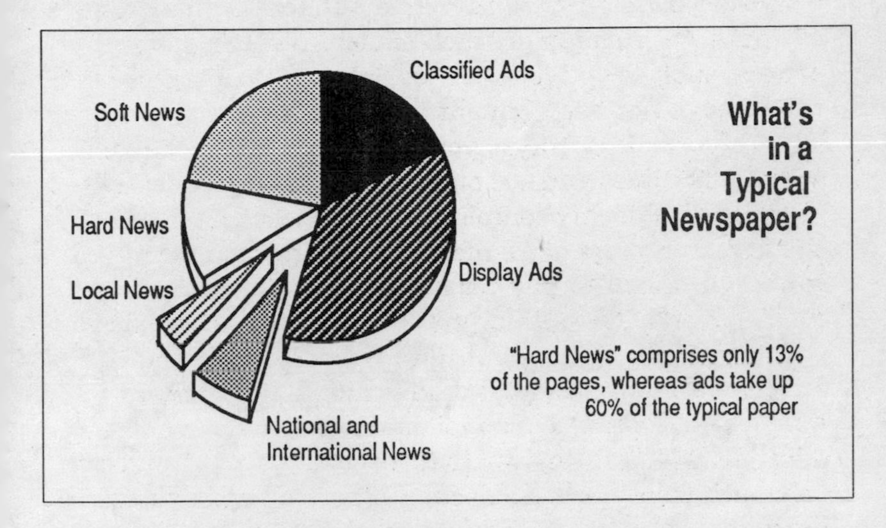

Similarly, if you appear on a TV programme for 4 minutes, you may find that 4 minutes of advertising time on the same programme would be worth £16,000.

None of it adds up to figures which would be defensible in a court of law, but the fact is that unpaid-for appearance on newspaper or magazine pages or in radio and TV programming is worth money. To you. To your product. Your charity. Or your company.

Researching Media Before You Start

- Before you paint a picture, you need to know how coarse the canvas is and how it accepts paint.

- Before you paint a wall, you need to know how big it is, whether it's on the outside of the building, exposed to rain, or on the inside, exposed to kitchen condensation.

Creating a public presence is somewhere between painting a wall and painting a picture, and before you start, you need some sense of the context in which you are working.

This is not an expensive business, but it *does* take a little time and a small outlay of money, because what you have to do is a preliminary analysis of the media through which you plan to disseminate your message.

Television

If you're doing your own publicity, it is unlikely that you stand a real chance of getting a story onto cable television, which tends to be pre-digested and heavily geared towards entertainment impure and simple.

But don't rule out any other TV networks on the grounds that they are too important and you too negligible. (Chapter 3 will help you work out just how negligible you really are, as a story, and how to tailor that story for specific media markets.)

A start-up company in the West of Ireland a few years ago got four minutes of wonderful exposure on BBC's *Tomorrow's World*. The company was making an unsinkable boat. No, not a latter-day *Titanic,* a one-person job for inland waters with much of its bulk infiltrated by expanded styrofoam. The *Tomorrow's*

World presenter had the time of his life, flailing around small angry Irish rivers and trying to make the thing sink. It wouldn't. He got a great item, and the makers of the little craft ended up with four minutes on video which they took with them to every prospective purchaser, because, look, folks, you don't have to believe *us*, just see what the Beeb said about our product.

But long before you can achieve a coup such as they pulled off, you need to have the canvas measured and explored. For that purpose, you need at least a television and preferably a video recorder—borrowed if necessary—with one of those gizmos which allows you to record particular programmes when you're at work, in the pub or tuned into another channel watching Kylie Minogue getting thinner.

In addition, you need the various magazines which give listings of programmes. These, at the time of going to print, include *Radio Times*, *TV Times*, *RTE Guide* and a couple of sporadic glossy outbursts concentrating on cable programming. By the time you read this book, that group are likely to have been joined by a publication listing the programmes on Ireland's new TV3 and, possibly, the programming on Century, Capital, 98FM and local radio stations throughout the country.

Finally, to complete this task, you need a highlighter pen, a notebook and a fortnight during which you will look at television programmes you would otherwise eschew, avoid and even deplore.

With highlighter pen in hand, identify the "content" programming on every relevant channel. If you are in Newry, that does not mean RTE is irrelevant to your purposes, and, contrariwise, if you are in Drimnagh, that does not mean that BBC Northern Ireland should automatically be ignored. Channel 4 is actively interested in material coming from Ireland, and other outlets should be noted as possible long shots, depending on the scale and importance of the story you want to tell.

For example, several of the overseas cable networks have shown an interest in material coming from Ireland. One cable has recently run a week long series of interviews with well known Irish people, and documentaries on various aspects of Irish life. The DISCOVERY channel, an off-shoot of the American cable of the same name, deals with factual, documentary type programming, and whereas it may, in the short term, be difficult to get something into one of those programmes, if you are seeking long-term publicity for yourself or your company, then you should certainly find out which independent production houses are providing DISCOVERY and other cable networks with their material. CNN, the news cable of Turner Broadcasting Systems, has its own little video ideas box, where if you happen to have your domestic video camera with you when a news event happens, you can make a (small) fortune by submitting it for their use. It follows from this that if you have someone with a relatively respectable video camera at a news event that you create, CNN just might consider looking at the resultant footage. Within a few years, it is safe to predict that the majority of TV stations will accept press releases and other programme inputs which are submitted on broadcast videotape in time for major "content-based" programmes.

By "content" programming, I mean the programmes which cover news, current affairs or community matters, live programmes coming from cosy afternoon studios, documentaries, magazine series which cover everything and specialist series, such as health or cooking, which cover only one topic. Locally produced drama series should also be noted, as well as game shows and panel programmes.

It sounds daunting. In reality, it is much less daunting, because television buys a great deal of its entertainment, its drama and its documentaries from overseas, and you do not have to pay attention to that.

The other programmes on your list you should now watch, with your notepad on your lap and a number of questions already scribbled on it.

Magazine programmes, whether specialist or generalist, and afternoon programmes, should be watched more than once, so you get a handle on the pattern and sequence of what gets on the air. When you sit down to watch this kind of programming, these are the kinds of questions to which you need answers.

Who's Presenting / Researching / Directing?

It may not matter to you who the sound operator or the vision mixer is, but it will matter very much that you know who are the presenters and who puts the programme together. Get the names down, and get them right. Get the titles down, and get them right.

If I am Ms Terry Prone, Director of *Afternoon Delight*, I will be less than gruntled to be addressed as Mr Terry Prone, fairly teed off if you post a letter to Ms Terri Prone, and straightforwardly vexed if you give me a title less important than Director. (If you give me a title *more* important than Director, I will be able to handle it, but the real owner of that title will not love you if he or she finds out.)

Don't ever tell a TV presenter or producer I said so, but I think researchers are often at least more important than either of the others. Researchers are always under pressure to come up with new ideas, with people who talk as if they were born and raised in TV studios, and with subjects so stimulating or emotive that the station switchboard is jammed for days with bellowing or weeping members of an inflamed public. The researchers are rarely treated with the respect they deserve, because many people eager to place an item on the airwaves believe you should "go to the top."

Making contact with a named researcher is much easier than making contact with a famous TV face or an eminent producer. A researcher is used to hearing half-formed ideas articulated, and may be very helpful in refining your thinking so that you present the idea in a tighter, more focused way.

If more than one researcher is credited in the programme guide as working on a particular show, make notes of all names. On a programme like RTE's *Late, Late Show* there may be as many as six researchers, some of whom will research anything, and some of whom will tend to favour particular subjects. There is always a researcher on such a programme with a particular affinity for the under-dog, whether that be the woman living in the streets and carrying her world in two carrier bags, or the community group opposed to the setting up of a chemical plant in their neighbourhood.

As you get more used to the PR business, you will begin to distinguish which researcher is likely to be more interested in your story. But you start by taking down *all* the names.

How long is the programme? How long are the sections?

In the programme guide, the programme may appear to be a half hour long. In fact, it is unlikely to be the precise thirty minutes. If there are many commercial breaks surrounding it or sandwiched within it, then the programme may be as short as 26 minutes.

Each magazine programme has a different favoured length for items to be included. Some go for three-minute limits, some stretch as long as ten. A rough timing helps in shaping what you are going to sell to a programme, and in preparing the speaker so that he or she does not deliver three minutes worth of material and then fill the remaining two minutes with increasingly discursive padding.

What's the Style?

If you expect all TV interviewers to be in the gutting and filleting business, then you may be at a loss when you go into a studio where all is ease and comfort, where the interviewer has no hidden agenda, and no upfront agenda, either, other than to hope you know what you're talking about and that you're prepared to expand on your subject when you are asked a warm and fuzzy question like "Tell me about this wonderful project of yours..."

So it is important to know the style of the programme. Look out for elements like:

Seating

Is it all soft and pastel and close to a middle-class sitting-room, or is it something between an interrogation zone and a classroom?

Involvement

Increasingly, even on news programmes, a strange chumminess breaks out, whereby the newsreader, the interviewer, the guest, the weather forecaster and, if you're really unlucky, the sportscaster, all get in on the act together and what passes for light banter goes on.

I once had a client, used to tough current-affairs programming, who went on an afternoon programme without having seen it in advance. The non-directive approval of the interviewer phased him for starters, because he went in braced for battle and got stroked affectionately instead. Then the programme's carpenter asked him something jocular about the kind of wood in the legs of his bed, and finally, the second presenter slid a lushly overweight cat into his lap and asked him to mind it while she explained the beauty of its pedigree.

"Open heart surgery without an anaesthetic would have been easier," he said afterwards. "Gawd, why didn't I look at the programme first?"

Patterns of coverage

If a programme has a cookery item every day, then there is no point in suggesting one to them. But if you happen to be pushing a new brand of pink courgette, the only virtue of which is its rosy hue, an item on it alone may not be possible, but the cookery expert might be persuaded to include it in a recipe. Getting publicity is often a matter of lateral thinking, but you can only do lateral thinking when you have something to be lateral against. So get a clear pattern of what their regular items are.

Viewership

By examining the time a programme goes out and the kind of item that goes into it, you can often get a fair idea of who sees it. Sometimes it is obvious. A programme that starts at three p.m. and finishes at four-fifteen is no use to you if you want to reach the business community or secondary schoolgoers. They are not at home unless they are in the sick minority. Sometimes it is less obvious. If you are trying to reach older people, it is easy to be misled into thinking they watch "older people's programmes". Quite apart from the shortage of specific programmes for older people, the fact is that older people watch and listen to a huge variety of programmes. Younger people, on the other hand, despite parents who constantly claim that their kids only watch nature and current affairs programmes, often, in reality, watch little but soaps and music shows.

Follow through

Some shows see themselves as having a public service function which is fulfilled, not just by broadcasting interesting material, but by making that material available in more than chat form. So they may interview you about your home for battered wives, and, at the end of the item, leave a caption onscreen for thirty seconds which gives the address and phone number of the refuge.

Or they may interview you about the significance of technical terms in food labelling, and then make available, on receipt of a stamped, self-addressed envelope, a leaflet which encapsulates your input. Or they may run a competition based on the subject you raised. Or they may insert supplementary information in the next edition of the glossy programme guide their station puts out every week.

Any one of these added value elements make more cost-effective an appearance on a particular show.

Space and Facilities

There are programmes appearing every week which can cope effortlessly with a brass band, a troupe of tap dancers, an action painter, a demonstration of weight-lifting gear, a couple of controversies, a comic and three harpists. If you tell the researcher for such a programme that you need to bring on a machine for assessing the presenter's cholesterol level, or show a videoclip, or present a model railway that covers thirty square feet and contains an artificial lake, the researcher may grit a tooth or two, and may even have to make arrangements for prop doors to be open and extra electricians booked to be present on the night, but he or she, if satisfied that the gadgetry is important, will be able to facilitate its use.

There are also programmes where there are no human camera operators in studio, where everything is done by remote control, and where the interviewer and interviewee are so close that a deep breath taken by one of them amounts to deprivation of the human rights of the other.

Getting a good sense of the physical scope at the disposal of a particular programme will prevent you developing unrealistic expectations of what you can achieve on that programme. (It is worth pointing out that a good straightforward interview in the claustrophobic studio may be more memorable than an appearance on a programme in which you are competing with a plethora of exciting unrelated items. It's a whole lot easier for an individual light to look impressive on a lampost than on a Christmas tree.)

When you have all of the information, it should be possible to work out, on the basis of your notes:

- What sort of items the programme might be persuaded to cover
- What length they might give the item
- What kind of angle they favour on a story
- Who, in the production team, would be the best person to approach with a suggestion
- What sort of pictures they need to make a story interesting for viewers.

Radio: National, Local and Community

Having done that for television, you need to move on and do it for radio. National radio networks carry hard news programmes. But they carry, in addition, a great many "soft news" or "features" programmes. Ideally, you should have heard the programme for which you might be suggesting an item. I remember once working on a programme whose presenter's name was gender-ambivalent. In other words, it wasn't obvious, from the moniker, what sex she was. It was a constant source of irritation to her and to the rest of the staff on the programme that people would telephone us, trying to sell us ideas, and reveal, as they talked, that they assumed her to be a fella, and clearly had never bothered to listen to what was, after all, our life's work at the time. The competing irritant was when people would ring up and say "Listen, I want to suggest that your programme give a bit of coverage to Topic A. I did try Pat Kenny's programme and Gaybo, but they're too filled up." No producer wants to think of his or her programme as Radio's Remainders Department.

If you are running a business and trying to get publicity for it at the same time, or running a career and trying to get famous, it is very difficult to spend hours listening to radio programmes. But there *are* other ways. All of us have friends who are addicts of one or another radio personality and programme type. Their brains are there for the picking. All of us have mates or pals who can be asked to listen to a particular show. Nor should we forget that there are media monitoring services in the Yellow Pages which tape and keep tabs on all sorts of programmes, so that if you want to hear what Terry Wogan's radio show is like, or what Gerry Ryan is currently doing, but cannot afford to tune in at the time they're on, then you can ring up the media monitoring company and ask them to send you a tape of a sample show. I have a friend who provides me with very precise help. A strange virus has confined this man, a writer by trade, to a wheelchair. He is physically limited, mentally unlimited. If I need to get the flavour of a programme series or of the output of a particular station, he will listen over a period of time and give me a report which is not only factually accurate, but which also gives me useful "steers" as to what may or may not merit inclusion in a particular programme.

Tracking the output of national radio stations in any country is relatively easy.

There are the publications which lay out weekly schedules and give considerable detail about individual programmes, such as *Radio Times* and the *RTE Guide*. Just reading through such publications tells you who's doing what, who the researchers are and whether the given programme is generated by the network's studio headquarters or a regional branch thereof.

Recent years have seen a great plethora of local radio stations taking to the air. The establishment of the Independent Radio and Television Commission in Ireland in 1988 saw the closure of most of the pirate radio stations which, up to then, had operated throughout the country. Since then, new stations have been set up all over the country and are continuing to be established. Although many of them major on music, all are obliged by law to broadcast 20% news and current affairs. This is a costly operation, and the local radio stations tend, accordingly, to be open to news items which are presented to them in a form which allows for easy use free of charge.

What that means is that any material going to your local radio station should be written in a way that another human being can read:

- Short sentences.
- Simple, rather than complicated concepts.
- First degree words (boat, book) rather than second degree words (vessel, tome).
- Images and examples that help the reader tell a story.
- Statistics used very sparingly.
- Big margins. Top, bottom and sides.
- Good white paper.
- Neatly typed, preferably using a big typeface like "Orator" or "Presenter."
- No paperclips joining page one and page two—it makes a noise in front of the microphone.
- No sentence running from page one to page two. Finish a sentence on page one. Start the next sentence on page two.
- Only the essentials included; keep the thing short.

In dealing with *one* local radio station, you have to know the names of the people who make the decisions about what's included, or left out of, programmes, and they have to know your names.

If you want to send something to *all* local radio stations, then you can get a directory of their names and addresses in Ireland from the IRTC. In Britain, local radio is longer established, and is served in a highly sophisticated way by a number of PR houses, which circulate taped items on, say, health and fitness, sponsored by companies making running shoes, which can be slotted into radio programmes free of cost to the station. The companies supplying these "instant content" items say that their monitoring indicates that the service is extensively used and is of great benefit to their clients. It is an idea worth exploring. There would seem to be some opening for the submission of sponsored material for magazine programmes, supported by companies which have a general corporate policy of being good citizens and which are therefore prepared to invest in taped material which has no direct connection with their own product or service. More directly linked material, such as recipes coming from a manufacturer of a specific ingredient, may raise ethical questions about free advertising or of advertising masquerading as disinterested objective material. The larger networks have their own policies about sponsorship, and many of them will let you have a copy of their guidelines. It can be very helpful if you are thinking about relating to local radio stations by means of material on audio tape.

Audio tape is relatively cheap, and An Post has a particularly cost-effective way of packaging and transporting taped material. It's called Cassette Post. It is my guess that in the future, press releases or versions of an announcement will go to the local radio stations on audio tape for direct insertion into programmes. It is certainly an area worth keeping a publicist's eye on.

The other emerging area is community radio, which has spread throughout the world, but has yet to make a major impact on Ireland, although the world body for community broadcasters is having its general meeting in Ireland in 1990. Definitions of community radio vary. In Denmark, for example, "community" is defined either as a geographical community or a community of interests. A community of interests might be the Christian community. Denmark finds it easy, because of its geography, to allow communities to relate to each other on the airwaves. In Copenhagen, there are more than twenty-five community stations, some of them sharing frequencies so that one group broadcasts at one time of the day, another group broadcasts later or earlier. Community stations tend to have a good deal of spoken word content, rather than music, and to focus on community consciousness-raising, local information and education.

In future, community radio will undoubtedly add to the opportunities and problems facing anyone who wants to publicise or solve public perception problems related to:

- An individual
- A new idea
- A product
- A political party or candidate
- An issue
- A company

Keep an ear on it!

Newspapers

Coming to terms with who does what on the national newspapers requires a little investment. Buy all of the national newspapers every day for a week, and set aside a minimum of two hours to analyse what you find.

The News Pages

These are the pages at the front of the paper, which deliver information on who attacked who, which country is fighting with which other country, what disaster has happened overnight, whose interest rates are rising and what the Budget says.

Look out, first of all, for *structure*. Note how the first paragraph of the stories is often printed across a few columns of the page, before the rest of the story continues in one column. Note also, how that first column is often printed in larger type and perhaps even in bold. (See pages 102 to 121 on how to craft press releases which meet this expectation.)

Look out for *content*. Some newspapers make front page leads out of stories which hardly appear in other newspapers, or which, if they do appear, surface in a half an inch on page seven. If you have a story to tell, you may have to resign yourself to the fact that it is much more likely to figure in one paper than in all of them.

Look out for *pictures*. Knowing what kind of picture an art editor goes for will greatly enhance your chances of placing a story that hinges on a linked photograph. One newspaper may favour pictures of children, joyous or plaintive. Another may favour pictures of young women, looking zesty, gleeful and sexy. A third may go for pictures of middle-aged intellectuals caught in a distance shot, surrounded by a great deal of white wall and hardwood flooring. You may choose not to go along with a newspaper's obvious preference—you may decide, for instance, that you're not going to collude with the zesty, sexy lady bit. But before you can make *any* judgements, you have to have the information on which to base the judgements; so look at the pictures.

The Feature Pages

These pages constitute the section of the newspaper which provides explanations or elaborations on the news stories appearing earlier in the same paper.

Here, you're looking, first of all, for the *regular*

columnists. Who are they? What do they write about? One may be a gossip columnist who spends her entire life at champagne receptions with people, famous for being famous, whose names appear in her copy heavily emboldened, so that social climbing readers pressed for time can hop from name to name. These columns are full of references to recent trips ("Suzy is just back from her Spring fortnight in Marbella, and sadly told me that the resort has lost the elegance it once had." They also have details of house purchases, sponsorships and wardrobes ("In her powder-blue wild silk...") Within the same newspaper may be a columnist who concentrates on expressing what are perceived to be national core values, and who, although he may allude to someone's success in print, is likely to add that the vital aspect of this success is that it hasn't changed Joe Bloggs a bit; he still eats jam sandwiches and takes his wife to the pictures once a week. There are columnists who adumbrate on the implications of a news story which happened earlier in the week, columnists who concentrate mainly on how badly television personalities or policians are doing their job, and columnists who start from a known standpoint (passionate feminism, socialism or advocacy of the Irish language) and work from there. There are syndicated columnists. Erma Bombeck appears in newspapers all over the world. Clever editors on this side of the Atlantic change some of the usages she favours which are particularly American, so they have her talking about biscuits rather than cookies, and petrol rather than gas. The end result is that she has been assumed to be Irish.

One client of mine some time ago got a strong notion that if he could just have a cup of coffee with Erma Bombeck, she would devote a whole column to his doings, and could I arrange for him to meet her in Bewleys?He was flummoxed to discover that she is based in America and was not expected, in the short term, to visit Bewley's. The moral is; don't waste time on columnists who are syndicated from other countries.

Dr Ruth is syndicated on sex. Countless cookery and gardening columnists are syndicated, too. On the basis of one week's reading, you can get a fix on most columnists" "hot buttons"; the subjects they are particularly interested in or handle particularly well. There are a few who escape classification, because of the variety of their preoccupations or because they write with tongues permanently in both cheeks. Once you have worked out where the regular columnists are at, the next thing is to look at the big features. These tend to break into two types. The first is what one national paper calls its "News Analysis" pieces; where front page stories are picked apart, explained and illustrated. The second is the examination of an issue which is less newsy, more permanent. So there may be features on skateboarding as an annoyance of modern urban life, on the expense of buying a decent kitchen, on the problems faced by MS sufferers, or on surviving Christmas without a) gaining weight, b) going bankrupt, c) fighting with your mother. In reading through these features, you want to know:

- How long are they? 800 words? 1,000? 1,200?
- How are they laid out? One newspaper at the moment may run a feature which has 1,500 words in it, but they won't be 1,500 continuous words. The main story will clock in at about 800 words, and then there will be little boxes set around that block of copy, some of them set in bold, some of them with pictures attached,which take individual aspects of the story, or which give the statistics in easy-to-understand chunks.
- Do they have pictures? Graphics?

- Are they heavy on quotations? Who are the quotations from?
- Are the features illustrated with the viewpoints of innocent by-standers from the street or are quotations from middling famous people preferred?
- Are any of the features personal viewpoints or experiences, written by someone who is not a journalist?
- Does the newspaper favour two- or three-part extrapolations of a central theme?
- Do the feature pages have regular "notification" slots where upcoming events, seminars, demonstrations and first meetings of new associations are flagged?
- Do the feature pages show a particular editorial bee-in-bonnet? Some features editors major on success stories involving travel, glamour figures and unexpected domesticities, whereas others prefer to focus on environmental, demographic or sociological themes which are not interpreted through the experience of one photographed person.

Any good PR professional, listening to a story from his or her client, can instantly say "This is one that the *Daily Snorkeler* will go for," or "No features editor would like this particularly, but the Head-the-Ball column would love it because it's so unusual." They can make instant judgements because of years of opening the paper hoping to find their client featured, and gradually learning the unwritten rules behind successful placement as opposed to rejection.

If you are planning to do your own publicity, you need to develop the same awareness, and you can only do this by watching, listening and reading.

The watching, listening and reading should go right down the line. Have a look at general magazines, and at the magazines geared for the market you're aiming at:

- If you are a charity, a general magazine, a woman's magazine or a young people's magazine may be relevant.
- If you are a small business, then business magazines and—depending on your product or your staff profile—women's magazines are a good target for stories about you.
- If you are a showbiz hopeful, then forget the business publications and go for the music rags or for the evening papers.
- If you are a budding politician, get in anywhere; you never know what media encounter will imprint a potential follower with your ideas or image.

The Tools of the Self-Publicist's Trade

If you are an actor who just wants the occasional mention in a gossip column, hopes that reviewers will spell your name right, and that the *RTE Guide* will *give* your name when the station broadcasts that play you wrote, then you have few needs, in publicity-generating terms, other than a hard neck and access to a telephone. So skip this section. If, on the other hand, you plan to do a professional job of publicising yourself, your cause, political group, charity or business, then a little investment is called for. What follows are the tools of the publicist's trade. One diamond beside the tool means it is an essential. Two diamonds mean it is not essential, but extra helpful.

◆ A telephone

◆◆ A facsimile machine (FAX)

◆ A typewriter

◆◆ A word processor

◆ Paper, letterheads, business cards, compliment slips, identifiable envelopes

◆◆ Someone at the end of your phone constantly

◆ A filing cabinet

◆ A way of accounting for publicity expenses

◆ An address book

◆◆ Membership of a professional organisation

Now, purchases you may be tempted to make, but which are not always worth the money they cost:

O A bleep

O A separate office in a posh building

O An elaborate photocopier

◆ A telephone

Is crucial if you're in the publicity business. You need to be able to reach people and be reached.

Obvious?

Uh, uh. One company which was rapidly and happily on the grow missed out on inclusion in a major positive series on TV about entrepreneurs because, although the company had an excellent phone system, it had not come to terms with the limitations of that phone system. Lots of people rang Brighteyes Ltd., and each of their phones would show by means of little lights how many lines were taken up. Often, when four out of the five were taken up, someone who wanted to make an outgoing call would casually lift the phone and absorb the last line.

On one particular day, this happened constantly. Every time the outgoing call was placed, an incoming call was stymied. Except that, on seven separate occasions, the incoming call that got the engaged tone was from a TV producer who wanted to make contact against a deadline. By teatime, he was hugely frustrated, and had decided that if they left their phone off the hook all day, Brighteyes could not be very bright. Brighteyes, of course, knew nothing of this and were choleric when they were left out of the programme series.

Moral; always have a phone system with slightly more capacity in it than you actually need, make sure incoming calls are answered within 5 ringing tones, and do not get in the way of wonderful curious outsiders who might publicly say agreeable things about you if they could just find you and talk to you.

No matter how big or small your office, each phone should have a 3M stick-on note pad beside it, and everybody connected with you drilled to take names and numbers accurately.

If you spend a lot of your time on the road, meeting people, one of those phones which allows your calls to be booted on to numbers where you will be is worth considering.

Remember that giving your telephone number to journalists is an irrevocable invitation that they should contact you. The first few times, it is flattering. Later, it may become invasive, which is why so many famous people have unlisted numbers. Think about it before you take the first step on a path you might regret.

◆◆ A facsimile machine (FAX)

Whoever invented the FAX is up there, in my estimation, along with the nameless heroes who invented the bed, the self disconnecting kettle and the word processor (See below).

A FAX is a wonderful machine which allows you to send letters to people in thirty seconds, run a script past someone in ten minutes, proof-read by remote control and run your business long-distance. If you are in the US, eager to unburden yourself of thoughts and it is in the middle of the night in Britain and Ireland, then, assuming the target of your thoughts has a FAX, you can send it off and it will be awaiting them when they arrive for work the following morning.

FAXes are a lot less costly than telephone calls, because there is no small talk, and a great deal of content can be transmitted very quickly. The FAX revolution means that every little copy and print shop has a facsimile machine, every post office will soon have one, and many large airports have several in their Business On the Move Centre. Large hotels have them, and in some cases, these operate on the same principle as a callbox phone; you insert your coins or your credit card, send the message, wait for a response and all is well.

Another advantage of these wondrous machines is that you get a printed record of who sent you messages and to whom you sent messages, with the duration of each telephonic encounter duly recorded, which is wonderful for your book keeper and your auditor. Faxes can usually photocopy in a limited way. By that I mean that they take excellent copies. Some of them produce better clarity than does a normal photocopier, particularly when it comes to black and white photographs, but they will only do it from an A4 page. If you want something photocopied out of a hardback book, you do not have the option you have with a photocopier, where you simply open the book and put it face down on the glass surface.

On the negative side, FAXes are quite expensive. The smaller versions have limited options, although my personal machine, which cost somewhere less than £1,500, uses my ordinary telephone line (you switch from phone to FAX depending on whether conversation or text transmission is your priority), allows me to photocopy, and churns out acres of material in my absence.

Negative, also, is the fact that FAXes can be used at this time, because of the absence of controlling regulations, by anyone who knows your number, as a way of marketing. Junk mail by FAX will undoubtedly become a problem in the future; indeed, it has been suggested that, because of the implied urgency of what it transmits, FAX takes away the power of refusal at the receiving end.

For a publicist, the FAX allows print material to go instantly to someone who may use it. One PR man working for a state sponsored body mentioned to me recently that he had mailed out a technical press release to his general press list of recipients, only to get an honestly plaintive phonecall from a newscaster at a local radio station.

"This looks very impressive," the newscaster said, "and I'd like to use it, but I'm not really sure what it means, and I'd be afraid to tackle some of the words—pronounce them, you know?"

"What time's your bulletin?" the PR man asked.

"Twenty minutes from now."

"I'll FAX you thirty seconds of script, OK?"

"Gosh, would you really?"

He really did, and the newscaster read it with as much warmth as if he were announcing the arrival of a permanent Christmas.

There are two major disadvantages to a FAX from the publicist's point of view.

The first is that, depending on the sophistication of the FAX at the receiving end, a pleasing press release may emerge on slimy warm thermal paper which develops shadowy finger prints if grasped by someone with warm paws. It can rob a communication of polish.

The second disadvantage is rather more important, and is the question of confidentiality. If you are sending a confidential document by FAX in a newspaper office, then you have to make damn sure that your chosen journalist is lurking beside the machine with her arms lovingly shading it from public view, or else your confidential material gets unconfidential very fast.

Confidentiality can also be kicked to ribbons if the person sending the FAX slips a cog. In Britain, in the week following an IRA bomb in Deal, which killed ten bandsmen of the Royal Marines, a two page FAX covering top secret changes in security at army bases was despatched accidentally to an employment agency. Less seriously, when I was collecting FAX messages sent from my office to an overseas hotel, I found included with those messages a three page stinker; a letter of complaint to the hotel from a recent guest which attacked the food, cast aspersions on the temperature of the water, the cleanliness of the floor, the civility of the staff and the honesty of the barmen. I returned it to the front desk trying hard to look as if I hadn't read it. But I had. And show me the human who wouldn't have, in the same circumstances.

So if you use a FAX, use it carefully, remembering that it is a much more open form of communication than a letter or a telephone call.

It is not essential that you own your own FAX, because of their wide availability in places like print shops.

◆ A typewriter

It has been said that in every journalist's bottom drawer is an unpublished novel.

I am convinced that in every writer and publicist's most cherished room is a typewriter smuggled across borders in wartime, buried in peat to prevent the Vikings getting at it and fed a typewriter ribbon around about 1913 which has been putting up a brave, if steadily paler, face ever since. There is a notion abroad that, like great brandy, the older your typewriter is, the better. There is a further notion that you cannot beat the old technology and that a good technician can keep an old typewriter going forever.

The last is sadly true. Bionic typewriters are everywhere, chewing circular lumps out of the paper every time the O key descends, and with oddly varied levels. For example, a Y may be a little higher than every other letter, with the result that text looks, for the most part, like a sprint with the Y in there going for the hurdles every time.

If you are going to write the Great Irish Novel or the Great American Novel, then an old typewriter may in some way support your muse, making you feel part of the great creative continuum which goes back to the moment when the first quill was wrenched from the behind of the first unsuspecting goose.

If you are in the publicity business, forget the creative continuum and get a good modern typewriter.

- Preferably an electric one which evens out your stroke so that the print is uniformly readable.
- Preferably one with a print head you can change about. This means a golf-ball (if you are buying second hand) or a daisy wheel. Daisy wheels are less durable. It is quite easy to knock a letter off one of them. But they are relatively cheap and easy to slot in and out. Having a variety of typefaces allows you to vary the material you are sending to people for purposes of emphasis.
- Preferably one which takes both fabric and carbon ribbon. The first can be used for all your routine or rough work, the latter for final fair copy going to journalists or impressing your Managing Director before you send it anywhere.
- Preferably one with a correction facility. Some of the newer machines have little screens where you can see the line you're working on before you commit it to paper, and correct as you go. Some have white tapes which pull an error off the page. One way or the other, publicity material thick

with dabbed-on Tipp-Ex is unacceptable.

- Preferably one which can be upgraded to a word-processor, see below.
- Preferably one you can use. If you cannot type, learn. Two finger typing is splendid in old Ben Hecht movies and unsatisfactory when it comes to doing a professional modern publicity job.

◆◆ A word processor

A word processor, like any addiction, is dead easy to manage without until you have got used to it. Once you have got used to a WP, everything else is slumming.

They start at about £600 and go up to several thousand pounds. If you want a laser printer which feeds out pages looking as if they have been printed and does it like lightning, that means you want a more expensive WP. If you want software that will give you natty little drawings and the capacity to do grids and charts and other pleasing visuals, ditto.

What a word processor does is let you see what you have typed before you print it out, thus permitting you to correct mistakes and to move paragraph three up above paragraph two when you realise that your sequence of storytelling is choppy. A good WP will tell you how many words you have in any one document, and will check the spelling of each of those words quicker than you could mis-spell Jack Robertson. It will alert you to the over-use of a word or phrase. **It will facilitate you in emboldening particularly important chunks of text so your readers pay extra attention**. It will do sums for you, put a date on your work, tell you the time and remember the phrases all of us have to use every day, like "yours sincerely". These it will type in at a keystroke, saving you time and tedium. If you go to the class end of word processors, your machine will also accept computer software, so you can do your accounts and mailshots, and it will send text to another related machine by modem and telephone.

For a publicist, having a good word processor means:

- Easy corrections when your committee finally come to a consensus about their press release.
- Quick variations on a theme. 5 different spokespeople from your organisation each have to make a speech on the same theme in 5 different locations on the same day. You type the main text into your WP, and then tinker with pleasing tops, bottoms, quotes and jokes so that each covers the same ground, but one does it in verbal rugby boots and another in stilettoes.
- Storage. Last year, you did this wonderful promotion for Whosits Frozen Sausages on a Stick. Suddenly, Mr Whosit has surfaced, waving a scant few pound notes and evincing interest in your achieving twice as much publicity for him this year. You go back to your programme for last year, shake the dust out of the ideas you never got around to using and send them out to excite people about frozen sausages. While you're looking through last year's files, you find that The Street Cred programme couldn't handle the sausages story at that time because they were running a competition to find the biggest cucumber in the country and thought the two couldn't mix. But they *did* say to come back to them, so you reach for the phone and talk about sausages.

  (This has a disadvantage. Using a word processor mail-shot system, my own company occasionally circulates glad tidings about itself and its

Machines that take daisy wheels or golfballs can usually offer the facility of an Orator or Presenter typeface. (Similar to this)

Orator and Presenter are over-sized, to make life easier for speech-makers and radio script readers.

So if you're hoping that something will make it on to a local radio station, why don't you type out the 'mention' you're hoping for on this kind of typeface and the DJ will:

A) Notice it, because so few scripts arrive on the DJ's desk in this form;

and

B) Find it easier to use than normal type.

services. Following the release of the most recent of these, I had a plaintive phone call from a man who was tired of being called Personnel Manager on envelopes going to the multi-million pound business he owned. If he had not called, we might have gone on calling him Personnel Manager forever. Moral: update your lists and do not insult the recipients of your mail.)

◆ Paper, letterheads, business cards, compliment slips, identifiable envelopes.

Every editor in town can dredge up from the subconscious a recollection of an editorial suggestion which came handwritten on a weathered sheet of lined paper, and which gave rise to a great story. Good goods come in all sorts of parcels.

Nevertheless, even the brightest idea can look shoddy, if it is typed on a sheet of paper which has had to have an address and telephone number typed on to it before the typist got to the idea. It may be neatly done. It may be clean white paper. But, if the sender is a business, the broadcaster who receives the missive may say "Well, this can't be up to much or they'd be able to afford letter heads." If the sender is a charity, the red light which clicks on signifies a thought process like this: "Hey, if they're not solid enough to have a place of business and a letterhead, should I encourage people to send them money? Will they handle it right?"

If the sender is a politician, the message of a grotty little letter is akin to standing on a soap box with a scarf firmly draped across the mouth; the reception of the good news will be somewhat muffled by mismanagement of peripherals. And if the sender is a Budding Star, a journalist will feel it fair to assume that budding hasn't begun yet.

It doesn't have to be gaudy; it doesn't have to be expensive. You do not have to order 500,000 sheets to store in crates in your attic. But a well-designed letterhead allows your letter to speak for itself with a respectable clarity.

I have a personal prejudice against business cards but they are much used by people who swear by them. My friend Dermot has a beautiful tall leather bound book filled with plastic pockets, business cards for the storage of, and at the drop of a hint, will happily show you his collection. My friend Phil has a collection of porcelain eggs. I would rate the two, in business terms, about equal.

Compliment slips, on the other hand, I have a lot of time for, because they can help you economise on long letter writing. Let's say you're publicising the visit of an overseas expert on genetic engineering, and you have the farming editor of a national newspaper nuzzling gently at an interview with the visitor. To feed the interest, you courier to the editor a biographical note on the geneticist, and a sheet indicating that this man has developed a strain of wheat which needs virtually no fertiliser, so everybody's ground water can be free of nitrates if it ever moves into production. Having just talked to the editor, what you want to achieve is that this support material hits his desk within the hour. So you pen a couple of sentences on your compliment slip (which has your telephone numbers, home and business, on it, your FAX number and your address), clip the slip to the typed pages, and entrust it into the black gauntleted hands of a courier. You will, of course, keep a copy of all the material sent. Courier services have revolutionised business communication, but every now and again a cog slips.

Once, a highly confidential document went from my office to a bank for urgent delivery to a director of the bank. What neither the director nor I knew was that, come 4.30, anything marked CONFIDENTIAL and delivered to the Bank got locked in a safe, regardless of other messages (like URGENT, PANIC STATIONS) on the envelope. In this case, the director and I could communicate by phone, but nobody could get into the safe. Had I not kept a copy, a major crisis would have been caused. On another occasion, the courier, *en route*, encountered, one after the other and at some speed, a mud puddle, a moving bus and a stationary JCB. He came surprisingly well out of this. The document didn't.

Envelopes are neither here nor there unless you have a little money to spare. Sometimes an envelope which is readily identifiable as coming from a publicist is helpful to the receiver because he/she can quickly extricate it from general mail. Sometimes, a readily identifiable envelope results in delivery, unopene, into the waste-basket, on the basis that it is "more crap from PR hacks." Six of one, half a dozen of the other. You take whatever choice best suits your style, your story and your publicity objective.

◆◆ Someone at the end of your phone constantly

Trying to get publicity and being simultaneously unreachable is a contradiction in terms. If you are out on the road a lot, then a cellular phone is a wonderful, if somewhat costly option. It means that time spent at traffic lights can be fruitful, not frustrating—as long as you have one of those hands-free phones which allows you to carry on a conversation just as you would with a passenger in the car. Cellular phones are getting cheaper and more portable by the minute. They are *not* getting safer. The cellular phone is a little broadcasting station which is picked up by the person to whom the call is directed, and by anybody else who has the scanning equipment which allows them to tap into such calls. There are lots of people who do it "just for the crack", and there are *samizdat* directories for sale which give the frequencies of VIPs worth listening in to, either because they discuss shares going up or down, or because they have unorthodox love lives, choreographed on their portable telephone. If what you're talking about is not confidential and is not very important, a cellular phone is fine. If you are making a strategic leak to a journalist, or warning your Managing Director that his misappropriation of funds has been discovered and that the police are covering his building thicker than ivy, use an ordinary phone.

If you're a one-man or one-woman show, operating out of your home, and using your home phone number, then anybody at home can be your permanent presence. One designer I know works from a granny flat at the back of his parents' house. Ring the number and a crisp voice answers "Hello. This is BRUSHSTROKES. Can I help you?" Eight out of ten callers are seeking the designer son. The owner of the voice happens to be his mother, but she never says so. "Antoin is out on a shoot this morning, but we're expecting him back by three," she'll say. "Give me your number and I'll make sure he calls you straight away." She then takes name and number accurately and leaves a neat record of same for Antoin.

Two out of ten callers are looking for Antoin's mother or father. The majority of them have now got used to his mother's brisk approach and the use of his company name, although there is an occasional acquaintance who is daunted into saying "Wrong number. Sorry" and ringing off.

A telephone answering machine is a poor substitute for a human being. Many people, me included, get strangulation of the articulacy when told to speak at the end of the beep, and we either don't wait for the beep, so all that is recorded is our departure, or we blither, or we turn surly and either tell the machine what to do with its little self or cut the connection in defeated silence.

If you must have an answering machine, make it work for you *as a publicist*. Take time and trouble recording a message which is crisp, clear and to the point. Do it yourself or get a pal to lend a voice. Do not get cute or facetious—and check your messages immediately you return to your home.

◆ A filing cabinet

Every publicist should have a super accessible, easy to manage and easy to expand filing cabinet for the storage of documentation, ideas, invoices, photographs, slides, etc.

◆ A way of accounting for publicity expenses

You take a journalist to lunch. You FAX a press release to a client for confirmation. You photocopy a hundred page document. You book a make up artist for photographs. You buy a newspaper to check if your story appeared. You drop a note of thanks to the journalist who wrote it. You buy a stick of Pritt to enable you to display a recent cutting on a card.

All of these activities could be undertaken in one day, and if you have that kind of hassled day, you may well forget to take notes of the fact that virtually all of these expenses are what are known as "third party charges" and billable to a client. If you are doing your own publicity, then you must keep notes of such expenses to lay before the Revenue Commissioners at the end of the year in order to prevent them removing half your earnings.

There are all sorts of little diaries available to allow you to keep account of such expenses.

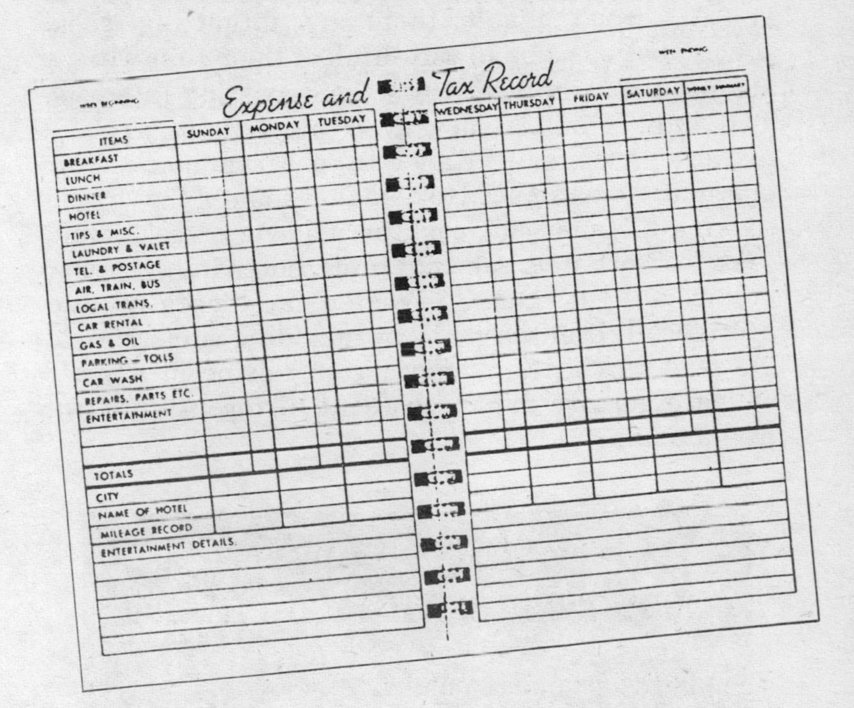

Expense and Tax Record

ITEMS	SUNDAY	MONDAY	TUESDAY	WEDNESDAY	THURSDAY	FRIDAY	SATURDAY
BREAKFAST							
LUNCH							
DINNER							
HOTEL							
TIPS & MISC.							
LAUNDRY & VALET							
TEL. & POSTAGE							
AIR, TRAIN, BUS							
LOCAL TRANS.							
CAR RENTAL							
GAS & OIL							
PARKING – TOLLS							
CAR WASH							
REPAIRS, PARTS ETC.							
ENTERTAINMENT							
TOTALS							
CITY							
NAME OF HOTEL							
MILEAGE RECORD							
ENTERTAINMENT DETAILS							

If you use a Time Manager or Filofax or version thereof, the chances are that there will be a section within the diary to facilitate record keeping. Whatever system you use, make sure you really *use* it, because otherwise, publicity can cost you a lot more than it is worth to you.

◆ An address book

A contact book is the single most important tool of a publicist's trade. It is what allows contact, quickly, with the right media people in an emergency. It is what ensures that you know who is who in every publication, and the direct line nearest their hand.

If you have not got a good memory, write down extra relevant details about the people you include so that you a) won't insult them by forgetting their preoccupations, and b) will think of them first when a subject comes up which fits their existing interests. The late John O'Donovan, a playwright who for decades presented RTE's letters programme *Dear Sir or Madam*, was amused to note that some of the writers seeking his miniscule cash prizes every week would seek to play on his personal preferences in literature, music and food, as revealed accidentally and sporadically over the years, by including a reference to his favourite writer, composer or cuisine in a letter which otherwise might be about hiring practices in Afghanistan.

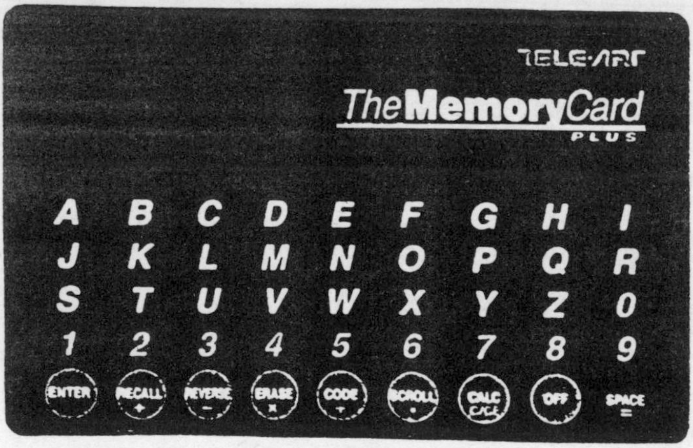

TELE-ART
TheMemoryCard
PLUS
A B C D E F G H I
J K L M N O P Q R
S T U V W X Y Z 0
1 2 3 4 5 6 7 8 9
ENTER RECALL REVERSE ERASE CODE SCROLL CALC OFF SPACE

It is now possible to use credit card telephone directories, which store up to 150 names but can be carried in a wallet. Make sure, if you go this route, that you have a hard-copy back up.

A friend of mine in the PR business left a folder containing his memory credit card on a radiator while he made a presentation, only to find on his return to the warm folder that the heat had made the card's innards go into spasm and it could never be persuaded to disgorge any number thereafter.

Contact books should be filled with sub-contractors who can be hauled in to handle specialist aspects of a job. Like who? Like photographers. There are photographers who are geniuses with still life. Give them a bottle of Irish Mist (as a prop, not for drinking purposes) a swatch of velvet fabric, a log fire and a couple of crystal glasses. The end result will be evocative and beautiful. Then there are photographers who are wonderful on fashion shoots. They can see what are the strong points of a particular garment or model, and create settings and moods which sell both. There are photographers who are great when it comes to doing corporate head-and-shoulder shots of the self-conscious who have been recently promoted.

And there are photographers who can move happily around a crowded reception, offend nobody, get good group shots and get the names of all within the group.

Your contact book should contain the names of several different photographers, with a note as to the specific strength of each. And it should do the same for designers, caterers, gimmick-producers such as the manufacturers of promotional umbrellas.

◆◆ Membership of a Professional Organisation

If you are a founder member of the Pig Tattooers Association of Europe, even if there are but a handful of international Pig Tattooers around, there can be an odd referred credibility accruing from membership of the Association, quite apart from the opportunities (which will be discussed in other sections of this book) of addressing the accumulated Pig Tattooers' Annual General meeting, featuring in social pictures at the Pig Tattooers Open Day, and being interviewed outside the European Parliament buildings as you lead a delegation fighting for the rights of pigs and their exterior decorators.

If you are a loner by nature, and have limited patience for committee meetings, minutes and minutiae, then you need to draw up a list of pros and cons before you join or create such an association. But bear in mind that there are some media fora which will listen to you with more attention as a disinterested association member or officer than they will if you appear with no other tag than your personal charm or company name.

Now back to purchases you may be tempted to make, but which are not always worth the money they cost:

○ A bleep

Bleeps are very exciting the first week, and after that tend to become irritants. You're always at the mercy of someone else's judgement—you just get requests to telephone someone, if it's a simple bleep, or instructions like "forget noon meeting" if it is a more elaborate one. You don't know what the someone wants and you have no idea why the meeting has been done in, unless you find a phone and ring the source of the information. Someone once described a bleep as "contact without power". And a meeting with someone whose chest pocket or hip whinges all the time and whose bleep has to be scanned every few minutes tends to be less than fruitful. Get a cellular phone. Or be like ET: phone home. Regularly.

○ A separate office in a posh building

While you are doing publicity on a small scale, you do not need a classy office. Most of your meetings will be held in your clients' offices, in the hallway of newspapers or over a meal or drink in a hotel. Nobody is going to judge your work by the depth of your carpet. Until you are sure of your market, and that you want to get seriously and major-league into public relations, stay put.

❍ An elaborate photocopier

There are photocopiers, these days, which turn out acetates for presentations, which collate endless copies of a complex 60 page document, which reproduce colour detail or actual colour photographs. They start expensive and go up to astronomical. If you are a one-person operation, you don't need a photocopier. Unless you live in the wilds, there is a copy shop in the suburbs near you. If you *do* live in the wilds, think first of a FAX machine, which for starters will put you in speedier contact with others, and will also give you small numbers of copies.

Only when that fails think about buying or leasing a photocopier and *read the small print of your agreement*.

5

What's Your Story? 101 Questions to Answer before Putting Words on Paper

In the next chapter, the mechanics of putting together a press release will be covered. But before you get to that point, you need to be sure that you have a story to tell that is worth the attention of journalists or the general public, and that you have identified what elements within that story make it attractive, or can be structured so it becomes interesting.

In order to do that, you need to stand back and question every assumption you may have about the story. The answers to these 101 questions will form the data on which your eventual press release will be based.

The first two questions are the most important. After that, the other ninety-nine follow in no particular sequence.

What's New about Your Story?

"Well, there's nothing very new about the story, I suppose. We've been doing the same thing for a long while now. But it's a very *good* thing and we do it really *well* and we're *nice* people."

Sorry, folks. Forget it. Routine worthiness is the reason for shooting the pianist and for not putting your name in lights. If you have always been doing this thing, then of necessity it is not news. And if it's not news, it does not earn inclusion in something which is called a *news*paper.

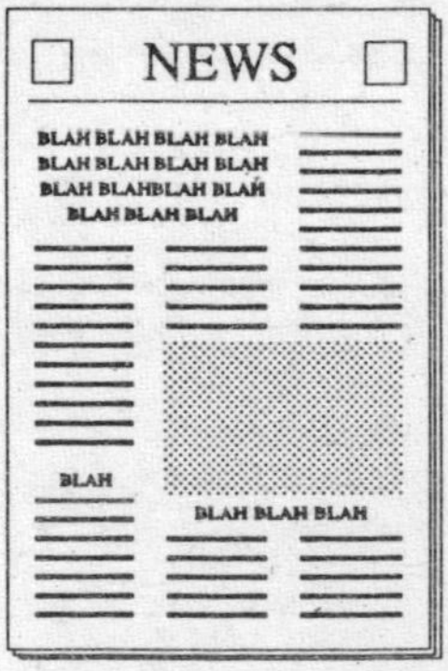

Journalists and broadcasters have no great sense of duty to individuals, groups or companies who—at least in their own eyes—make an important contribution.

The journalists and broadcasters have an overwhelming sense of duty towards their readers, listeners and viewers, all of whom can be assumed to have a short attention span and acres of other delightful things competing for their attention. So if all you have is a strong personal conviction of worth, do not go seeking publicity. Find something about your story which is new.

Someone once said that a writer's job was to make old things new and new things familiar. That's the job of PR people, too. They have to look at stories which have all the individual appeal of yellow pack soap on a conveyor belt, and discover something about those stories which can be parlayed into an angle.

Some of the later questions in this section may help you to do the same for your story.

What's Different about Your Story?

If, looking at your product, your service, your personal talent, your political party or your charity you cannot instantly find five or six crucial differences between it and every other operator in similar areas, then you have a lot of work to do.

In business terms alone, differentiation is crucial. As was underlined by economist Masanori Moritani, in his book *Japanese Technology*, where he says that:

> *One of the characteristics of competition in Japan is the establishment of small distinctions between one's own product and similar products made by other manufacturers. These tend to be minor improvements in convenience, function, miniaturization and the like... Five, six or even as many as ten companies may be producing virtually identical products, but upon close*

examination, you will find a number of small innovations in each. Since each firm is rapidly making such improvements in its goods, the cumulative effect is immense. In two or three years the product can be completely transformed.

People who buy hamburgers in McDonalds get a very different kind of hamburger, *they believe*, from the hamburger people get in Burger King. People who buy a Honda car have a clear notion of what differentiates their Civic from someone else's Ford Fiesta. People who refuse to consider a computer other than an IBM differentiate IBM from all other suppliers.

Differentiation helps you sell. But it does more than that. It can create a strong sense of corporate identity, so that staff are proud to work for the X company as opposed to the Y company, which, on the face of it, produces very similar machinery. And it can help in achieving publicity, because journalists are curious about the company which has such a strong sense of identity.

Sometimes, the people within a company are not the best differentiators. A couple of years ago, a group of us within Carr Comunications were doing a brainstorm as to what made us different from and better than everybody else. (We were ignorantly arrogant; we figured we were better, it was just a matter of getting the evidence together.)

A client unexpectedly dropped in, and when I went out to thc lobby, I told him he was interrupting a most important corporate exercise.

"The audit?" he asked.

"No," I said."We're just trying to work out points of difference between us and all the other PR companies."

"I can tell you what they are," he said. "You're the no-bullshit PR agency." (Out the window went words I had hoped to hear applied to us, like "prestigious")

"Go on," I said, taking pen in hand.

"You don't have waiting rooms filled with soft carpet and classy magazines and mahogany tables. You don't give people cups of coffee in good china. You don't have note pads with your corporate logo on them. But anybody who comes in that front door gets a sense of excitement and buzz and fun. Whatever staff member comes through the lobby will give chat to anybody who's waiting, and there's a general lack of subservience that I like. And don't get any ideas about charging me more money, because I'm bloody well not going to *pay* for getting my coffee in a big red mug."

I went back to my group and suggested that although we may prefer phrases like "corporate strategists *par excellence*" to make us feel important and different, what our clients actually perceived as making us unique was quite different. Your clients can tell you what is different about your operation (negatively as well as positively) but it is vitally important that they like the difference.

Tom Peters, one half of the *In Search of Excellence* team, in his bestseller *Thriving on Chaos*, (Knopf, New York, 1988) stresses this point.

> *Don't forget that it's not differentiated until the customer understands the difference. Sometimes a new idea is on target but still is not "sold"—i.e., communicated—effectively. Scandinavian Air Systems's Chief, Jan Carlzon, tells of a fare-reduction campaign launched years ago at the Swedish domestic airline, Linjeflyg. The programme was called "F50" to indicate fares at an attractive 50% off. But F50 flopped. When Carlzon took over the airline, he retained the idea, but renamed it the "Twenty Dollar Plan", signifiying the actual fare. the switch from*

technical argot to plain talk caused the programme to catch fire. Carlzon explains "What people don't understand doesn't exist."

The differentiation process applies even if you're simply in the business of publicising your personal self. Let me give you an example.

In my late teens, I joined the Abbey Theatre as a student actor. At the time, student actors were required to learn voice production, understudy parts they would never have a chance to play, run errands, sit in the prompter's box until cobwebs were constructed from their ears to the wall, be humble and adoring in the presence of all "real" actors, directors, writers and stage managers and hope that one day someone would drop dead and they'd get their big break. Within the Abbey building are two theatres, the Abbey and the Peacock, and, at the beginning of the Theatre Festival one autumn, there was a major flurry of publicity, generated by one of the company directors. One day, journalists and photographers from newspaper after newspaper came in to take pictures of almost everything and every performer. Except me.

Now, I had learned the lesson that a young actor's place is underfoot, that a woman's place is in the wrong and that if you are pushy you can Get a Reputation. Nevertheless, my blood began to boil, and as I hauled props into position for photographs which would exclude me, I began to have heavy duty bad thoughts. Dammit, went those bad thoughts, you've been here a while and you're working like a dog and if you don't appear anywhere in any of these stories you are going to be seen as a talentless slave.

Attacking the director who was playing host to all of these visiting journalists was not going to pay off. So I watched what was going on. No very special stories were being generated. Just "Here is a rehearsal in progress for the show upstairs in the Abbey this week," and "Here is an actor from the show downstairs in the Abbey this week." The reason I did not figure in either set of pictures was that although I appeared in both shows, my parts were minuscule.

Hold it... I appear in both shows, I told myself. I am the only one who appears in both shows, I gurgled silently. I'm in for three minutes at the beginning of *Borstal Boy*, playing the woman whose IRA son gets caught bombing something, and then I wipe the tears off, pull off the dingy apron, get a pair of high heels and a short skirt on, and get into line to sing the opening ditty in the revue that has a later curtain up time in the lower theatre.

When the photocall finished, I crossed the river to the office of the *Evening Press*, where I had a journalistic acquaintance, and, trembling both at my own temerity and at the possibility of later retribution, told him that I had a great story for him. That evening, the rehearsal pictures ran on an inside page, and the picture of me, the girl playing in two theatres, ran on the front page. (Retribution never happened, either. The director who had never noticed me up to then, decided that I must have a bit of backbone and gave me better parts. Still minuscule, but better minuscule.)

Find points of difference between your story and everybody else's story, make sure everybody on your side knows about those points of difference, and, when others start to copy you, keep moving and inventing new subtleties to distinguish you from everyone else.

What Does Your Product or Service or Charity Do That Others Don't?

Several years ago, two policemen came to see me. Detectives, to be more precise, and deeply threatening because of role and size—both of them being the kind who would only have to lean gently on a criminal to make said criminal wilt.

They were involved in a charity and they wanted guidance as to how to get publicity for their fundraising efforts. As they saw it, they were looking for research money for cancer and that was enough. No, we told them, it was not enough. Research is a concept which does not make people reach eagerly into their pocket to find money for disbursal purposes. "Research" always sounds like you're giving an academic a job for life playing with Petri dishes and looking down microscopes. "Cancer" is often heard as a great big threatening shapeless threat. C'mon lads, we said (getting over our fear that they would read us our rights or say "Book 'em" to each other) what problem was this charity going to tackle that wasn't already being tackled by a million others?

"Well, it's bone cancer," one of them suggested tentatively.

Suddenly, the other man got mad.

"I'll tell you what it's going to tackle that nobody else is tackling," he said. "This is a bone cancer that strikes kids, right? Kids in their teens who could grow up to be athletes or dancers. And if it's caught in time, a whole massive bit of the kid's body has to be taken out. Right? And in the past, that was it. If it was an arm, there would never be any use of the arm again. If it was a shoulder, not only would there be very little movement, but the distortion of the kid's frame—can you imagine? And now, not only is the surgery improving, but research is coming up with prosthetic limbs that can be put in instead of what is taken away and there are marvellous success rates and the young people go on to live a decent normal life. Right? *Right?*"

There was a stunned silence.

"But we can't say that," the other detective said.

"You can't? Why can't you?"

They looked at each other. (It was easier than looking at us, who were so much lower on the ground than they were.)

"I suppose if the surgeon didn't mind..." one of them speculated.

"Possibly, if we could present it in a way that wouldn't hurt any of the teenagers that have had the surgery," the other nodded.

One of our staff, who has shorthand, read aloud from her notebook the transcript of the detective's outburst. With a couple of tinkerings here and there, it became the framework of the story that the two men told, which earned the charity a fortune.

A few years later, the two came back. They were embarking on another fundraising effort, and wanted to generate publicity for it. "Now, let me tell you what this fundraising is going to do that isn't being done by anyone else," one of them began, beaming.

What Makes the People in Your Company or Organisation Newsworthy?

Just as there is guilt-by-association, so there is image-by-association, too. So ask that first question, and follow it up with these:

- ❑ Has any staff member worked with a world-famous name?
- ❑ Or been part of an arctic expedition ?
- ❑ Or survived an outbreak of Legionnaire's disease?
- ❑ Or qualified in some brand new science?
- ❑ Has a staff member discovered a new oil well?
- ❑ Or won an award?
- ❑ Or changed career radically?
- ❑ Has a staffer invented something or discovered something?
- ❑ Developed a new area of expertise?
- ❑ Researched something in a way that casts new light on it?
- ❑ Does any of your staff have an oddball talent? (tongue-twisters or puns or part-time puppetry).

If any of these questions provokes a positive answer, then you may have an unexpected method of attracting attention to an otherwise unstartling story.

Ask questions of yourself and other key members of the operation, including:

- ❑ Are you an emigrant, coming home and starting something new?
- ❑ Are your academic qualifications oddly at variance with what you are doing now?
- ❑ Is your work experience in any way unusual?
- ❑ Did you do something else interesting before?
- ❑ Do you hold to any unusual creed, eating habit or health regimen?

  (Let's look at it this way. If you manufacture babies' rattles and, for private leisure pleasure, are in to kick boxing, the contrast could give rise to quite a story.)
- ❑ Have you ever been acknowledged by an association or validation group as being special in any way in the performance of your work?
- ❑ Do you have a new partner?
- ❑ Are you a workaholic?
- ❑ What hours do you work?
- ❑ Are you married to the managing director?
- ❑ Do you have a specific area of expertise arising from your career?

  (Whether you cook, doctor, DIY, solicit [in a legal sense] mend cars or grow things, you may have an area of expertise which could be useful to a radio or TV programme, with spin-off value to your core business.)
- ❑ Is this a family operation now changing to be a non-family operation?
- ❑ Do you employ part-timers or have you invented some interesting variant on flexi-time?

- Do overseas academic institutions send students to spend time learning the ropes with you?
- Are you the rescuer of a moribund business?
- Do you employ more young people than average?
- Or more old people?

  (Don't knock it as an interesting trend. See below, page 138.)

Any movement of people within an operation should give rise to interesting story "hooks", if you ask questions about them:

- Is anyone being promoted?
- Is a staffer setting up an associate company with backing from the parent company?
- Have staff set up anything like Quality Circles?

  (Quality Circles is a Japanese method of improving workforce commitment to quality by means of structured weekly meetings run to very specific guidelines.)
- Do you have an oddball incentive or ideas scheme which allows staff to talk back or contribute to the direction of the company or organisation?
- If you're planning an expansion, will you be hiring a particular number of people from a particular discipline in the near future?

  ("Rural firm to seek 5 Elephant Propagators")
- Are any of your staff taking a year off, with your support, to work in a third-world country?
- Is someone retiring whose work history is fascinating?

  Long years ago, when I was presenting a radio magazine programme, a department store manager rang me up. He wanted me to interview his Mr X, who was retiring as Manager, Floor Coverings.

"Floor coverings?" I said, in a voice reeking with disbelief and rejection.

"Floor coverings," he said with total confidence. "Yes, I know you think it's the most boring subject in the world, but it isn't. Floor coverings have a fascinating history. Even linoleum, although there isn't that much of it around these days, has natural woods and resins in it that allow it to absorb germs from the air so it is particularly useful in sickrooms. Some floor coverings allow static electricity to build up. Some of them invite accidents. This man came into this shop when he was fourteen and he's worked in Floor Coverings ever since and I think you will find him a great addition to your programme."

You could see my reservations a mile off, but I caved in and allocated three and a half minutes to the flooring man. The item ran to ten minutes and I got letters reproaching me for cutting him off just when he was getting into his stride. A magazine writer who heard the item subsequently interviewed him, too.

- ❑ Do you send your staff on any particularly unusual training courses?
- ❑ Have you any special arrangements for personal
- ❑ Have you any unusual creche or nursery provisions?
- ❑ Do your people wear a uniform and if so, are you planning to update or re-design it?
- ❑ Do you have any unusual rules—like banning memos because they are self-derving?
- ❑ If you are a multi-national, do you send your staff for experience to the parent-company?

- ❑ Are there any hero stories to be told about your staff?

There is a freight company based in Dublin which makes the usual claims for speed, service and variety of haulage equipment. But talk to its Managing Director, and he will immediately start telling you about the time one of the company's clients had a fire at its manufacturing plant.

"Our drivers just heard about it on the grapevine, and literally within minutes, without our ever calling on them to do it, they were arriving at the plant and taking out stuff from areas the fire hadn't got to, loading it onto the trucks and getting it off-side. They weren't asked to to it. They weren't paid to do it. It wasn't their own employer whose goods were threatened. But they just moved in and saved hundreds of thousands of pounds worth of stuff. It's something the lads still talk about when they get together, and it's something we're all very proud of."

In the security business, Securicor is a household name. It's their job to carry loads in armoured cars and make sure that not a penny gets lifted. But that's not to say that the company doesn't celebrate the occasions when staff are put under special pressure and handle it particularly well. One of the classic examples happened to the crew of a Securicor armoured vehicle. But let's have Securicor tell the story.

"On the 12th of July, 1988, an eight-man gang mounted an elaborate, well planned attack on a Securicor van in Cabra. The van, on its way to Cabra Social Welfare Offices, was rammed by two stolen cars at Glenbeigh Road, at 8 a.m. A JCB digger then moved in immediately and turned the trapped van onto its side. Two of the men, wearing balaclavas and shouting threats, proceeded to rake the windscreen with heavy rifle fire, but failed to penetrate the vehicle. Efforts to prize open the escape hatch also proved unsuccessful and the gang was forced to flee empty handed.

Throughout the attack the Securicor crew remained calm and managed to contact the Gardai. The Securicor three man crew was awarded the Irish Security Industry Bravery Award in October, 1988."

These calm men were heroes. Getting publicity for their heroism was relatively easy—especially since there were pictures.

- Have your staff got any special experiences or insights about which they might write in trade or other publications?

Once you are satisfied that you have examined the publicity potential implicit in your staff from every possible angle, move on to ask questions about other aspects of your business.

Premises:

- Is there anything unusual about your headquarters?
- Are you the first tenant in a brand new building?
- Have you sensitively restored an old building?
- Is yours the first plant of its kind in this country or this continent?
- Was your establishment once lived in or visited by some historic figure?
- Have you a ghost?
- A secret passage?
- A sick building that got cured
- Are you moving to bigger or better?
- Are you renovating the building?
- Extending it?
- Putting in solar panels or other environmentally friendly plant enhancements like segregated waste storage areas (paper, glass, garbage)?
- Fighting to put up a sign outside it?

  I kid you not. The building where I work is precluded by an odd commingling of competing interests and by-laws from putting up a large sign saying HERE WE ARE, STOP AND BUY ONE or words to that effect. The oddity of where the building is situated means that one client came from his base, 300 miles away, and never found us at all, going home to his headquarters defeated and convinced that as a business we needed to do a bit about promotion. He was right, of course, but all we could do was get a foolproof map designed and sent to visitors in advance of their arrival.

Finances:

- ❑ When is your AGM?
- ❑ Are your profits going up or down?
- ❑ Are you going to take over or be taken over or diversify or pull out of diversification?
- ❑ When will you issue your annual report and how can it be differentiated from all the other expensively produced self-stroking documents issued every year?
- ❑ Is one area of your business suddenly doing particularly well?
- ❑ Has a bank taken a stake in you?
- ❑ Are you seeking venture capital to embark on expansion, and if so, what is the direction of the expansion?
- ❑ Are you going to go public?

Your product or services:

- ❑ Do you use any odd methods or materials?
- ❑ Do you supply an unusual market?
- ❑ Where did the idea for your product come from?
- ❑ Are you packaging it in quite a different way?
- ❑ If it is something with a limited shelf life, how

have you extended that shelf life?

- ❑ Are there any inducements to buy?
- ❑ If a customer buys fifty packets of your product, will he or she win a holiday in Iceland?
- ❑ If a retailer sells fifty packets, will he or she get a plaque for the shop wall?
- ❑ Does your product meet any special needs? (food suitable for people who suffer from a particular illness, hand tools for people limited by arthritis, alarm clocks with a terrifying sound designed to wake people who would sleep through the last trumpet, or packaging geared to prevent opening by toddlers.)
- ❑ Do you sell direct or by mail order?
- ❑ Do you sell over the counter in shops or have you found a different approach?

When the people who invented Mrs Field's Cookies in the US started to sell their product, they realised that they had to overcome people's normal expectations about cookies (biscuits, to us on this side of the Atlantic). Cookies were expected to come in packages sealed at the factory, and to be hard and cheap. Mrs Field's cookies, on the other hand, were big, soft, irregular, put into bags in twos and threes only when the customer had chosen them, and were decidedly not cheap.

The Mrs Field's cookie people realised that customers were going to have to be wooed into coming into a cookies-only shop where this quite different product was on sale. So they cut up cookies into bite sized pieces, scattered them on a plate and entrusted the plate to a staff member who went out into the shopping malls to wander and offer samples to window-shoppers. Having tasted, for free, the goods, the customers came in droves.

- ❑ Are your sales confined to one particular time of the year?

  (If you make Christmas crackers or Easter eggs or swimsuits, they are.)

- ❑ Are there major threats or opportunities facing enterprises like yours in the coming decades?

Your method of production:

- ❑ Are you particularly "green"?
- ❑ Do you operate "just in time"?
- ❑ Have you taken on board any methods from other countries?
- ❑ Do you do your own R&D?
- ❑ Do you avoid testing on animals?

  Anita Roddick of THE BODY SHOP created an internationally identifiable company profile and brand image out of the last two elements above. Then, just as the uniqueness of those claims was beginning to wear off, she began to let the public know about THE BODY SHOP's attitude to staff, profits and customers.

- ❑ Do you meet particularly exigent standards?

  Let's say you produce some kind of pharmaceutical product, and not only does it meet European standards, but it meets the USA's FDA standards, too. Do not go looking for bushels to conceal this under.

- ❑ Have you been accorde "vendor" status by some classy multi-national?

  Robert Spencer's Strongbow engineering company, in Waterford, is in the business of making complicated metal bits for the insides of computers—and sometimes complicated metal bits for the outside of computers. Since the company had gone through a number of bad years before he took it over, it was a priority with Mr Spencer that the vaguely bad connotations be sheared away from the Strongbow name. The key factor in letting him achieve precisely this aim was when two multi-national computer manufacturers gave his company their ultimate

Irish Independent, Monday, September 18, 1989

Editor Brendan Keenan

Grapevine

Stringing a bow

Three years ago, no-one wanted Strongbow Engineering. It was ready to be sold out as scrap and the State's investment written off.

Robert Spencer, the current managing director met Hugh Cooney the receiver of the business and offered to lease the equipment with an option to buy.

In those intervening three years Strongbow has been pulled back from the brink of disaster with a healthy thriving order book.

Exports amounting to 25 p.c. of its turnover which is projected to be almost £2m next year, up from £548,000 in 1988.

Last year Strongbow was awarded ship to stock status by Digital and Concurrent Computer and by Wang in 1987 imprimatur; ship-to-stock status. For non-computercrats, what that means is that a vendor—in this case Strongbow—is authorised to deliver its wares without checking at the receiving end. It means that the purchaser—Wang or Digital—trusts and values the supplier and chooses to deal with them in preference to others. Robert Spencer made damn sure that this corporate pat on the back got noticed and flew UK journalists into the plant to show them too.

- ❑ Are there users of your products or services who are well known?

  Many a designer has become a household name, not because of publicity sought directly, but because some famous person appeared at some much-photographed event in a little number created by him or her.

- ❑ Do you export any of your product?
- ❑ Do you ever have shortages of a particular raw material?

  Yes, a shortage can be made into a positive news advantage. See Case History; Daffodils, pages 160 to 170.

- ❑ Is there anything particularly risky about what you do or make?

  If there is, then don't hope that keeping your head down will solve your problem. Be upfront, and indicate precisely not only where you meet all the existing safety standards, but how you exceed them. (If you don't *exceed* them, get into the exceeding business quickly and stay in it.)

Your Company History, Management, Style and Stance:

- ❑ Have you ever had bad times?

  One of the great mistakes PR people make is to position their produce or client relentlessly on the sunny side of the street. It gets awfully boring. People's failures and hassles are much more interesting to the rest of us than a parade of their successes. Not to mention the fact that the admission of mistakes and the implication that one learned from them is a common trait of highly successful people, as identified by a Gallup poll. Survival always makes a great story. (Non-survival sometimes makes an even better story, but it tends not to be autobiographical.)

- ❑ Have you prevented a disaster affecting other producers of similar goods?

- ❑ Have you coped well with an emergency?

  The way the Tylenol people coped with the scandal emerging from the sabotage poisoning of their product by some nameless psychopath did the brand name enormous good. Similarly, on a much smaller scale, some little businesses producing food items like pates and mayonnaises did quite well out of recent botulism and listeria scares, by establishing how safe their products were rendered by a particular technology.

- ❑ Have you got interesting directors?

  And if not, why not?

- ❑ Who established the corporate culture in your organisation and what is it like?

  Every organisation has a different flavour to it. Some managers are not aware of the elements making up the "corporate culture." Some are. If you are into consensus management or the promotion of disadvantaged groups, or the abolition of mandatory retirement at sixty-five, there may be a publicity angle in your internal realities.

- ❑ Do you have policies about, say, taking on an extra person to your staff for every extra £X of turnover?
- ❑ Do you have links with similar bodies overseas?
- ❑ Do you commission research into how you're seen in the marketplace?
- ❑ Do you commission research into any aspect of what you do?

  If you make pills, a study on patient compliance may be interesting to the public. (Patient compliance is how well patients obey their doctors when they tell them to start taking the tablets, and if the tablets have unpleasant side effects, patient compliance gets thin on the ground.)

Your Community Profile:

- ❑ Do you contribute to the community in which you are based, other than by providing some jobs?
- ❑ Do you or your colleagues donate time or materials or money to charities, youth organisations or civic projects?
- ❑ Does your company contribute to the company in a public way?
- ❑ Do you offer "open days" at your plant?
- ❑ Do you supply local schools with educational material about your operations or educational

material shorn of direct commercial tielines?

- ❑ Do you have staff "days out"?
- ❑ Do you or your colleagues make speeches at conferences?

  (If you do, make sure you do it well. A useful book is Terry Prone's *Just a Few Words*, from Poolbeg. Since you asked...)
- ❑ Do you contribute interesting features on aspects of your business to specialist magazines?
- ❑ Do you write thought-provoking features on the economics of your business for national newspapers?

  It doesn't matter whether you're in fundraising or politics, a good feature which stimulates discussions or lets readers in on secrets is always an attention-getter. And, since you press me, I have to admit that the book you probably need to get you started on such feature-writing is Terry Prone's *Write and Get Paid for It*, from Poolbeg.

6

How to Write a Press Release

A PRESS release is a publicity device which, if crafted well enough, may end up being printed in a newspaper with practically no alterations.

But that is not the only way it can do its job for the sender.

- *It may trigger a bigger story.* An editor, reading the release, may decide he wants an angle on the theme covered, and send a reporter out to get lots of extra information.
- *It may trigger a profile.* The press release may be about ice-pop sausages, but a magazine writer may decide that the mind and lifestyle of someone who could dream up such a product would be more interesting than covering the product itself.
- *It may trigger a series.* Victor Hugo said that no army could withstand an idea whose time had come. A press release which happens onto an editor's desk when she's thinking about a similar topic can be precisely that idea.
- *It may trigger an interview.* A radio programme may have no interest in straightforward new product announcements. It may have a pattern of strange-but-true interviews carried on in a facetious way by a DJ, and may be attracted by the sausage story to invite the inventor on the show.
- *It may trigger a mention.* There are sections in every newspaper and magazine where small gaps happen, and gobble up any available copy. A columnist short of copy may do an "I see some bright spark has come up with an odd product" story, or a desperate sub-editor may lift the top paragraphs of the story and run it in an inch long "filler".

There are never any guarantees. The day you issue your release may be the day that three jumbo jets collide over Devon, or Florida is swept away by a hyper hurricane, in which case obscurity will be the fate of your release. File it, lick a wound or two, and when you have another opportunity, tinker around with the wording and the headline so nobody will spot it as a re-cycle, and send it on its way again.

What you must remember, when you set out to write a press release, is that every newsdesk in the country is swamped by hundreds, if not thousands of press releases every day from:

- Government Departments
- Commercial firms
- Voluntary and community groups
- Activists (for example Greenpeace)
- Showbiz personalities
- Public services

  (Your water is going to be cut off / there will be a diversion in the city centre / if you want a policeman, this is the new number...)

- Other publications / programmes

  (Believe it or not, a magazine may send a press release to a newspaper or radio programme or both in order to get attention for a major feature in this week's issue. Or a TV station may be seeking publicity for a programme series being launched.)

Some of those press releases are crisp and to the point. The majority are too lengthy, too florid and too discursive. Any sub-editor will tell you that the man or woman at the receiving end infinitely prefers something short, rather than something long. Additional information is always easy to come by, and so a single-page press release which outlines the saga in terse monosyllables is always popular at a newsdesk, whereas a five page sawn-off version of the *Encyclopaedia Brittannica* is hated.

A good press release is shaped like a comet. Thus:

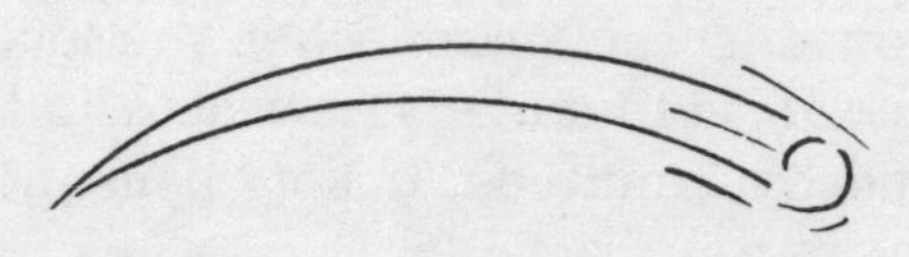

The shorter the tail, the better, but that does not mean you should overload your lead.

The lead in a release is the paragraph which, all on its own, tells the essentials of the story. Traditionally, journalism students were taught that the questions

What?

Where?

Who?

When?

Why? and

How?

should all be answered during the first paragraph of a news report. Therefore, by implication, the same six questions should be answered in the lead paragraph of a press release.

Kipling's Questions

I keep six honest serving-men
(They taught me all I know)
Their names are What and Why and When,
And How and Where and Who.

I send them over land and sea
I send them East and West
But after they have worked for me
I give them all a rest...

So the lead paragraph in your press release might go like this:

FROZEN SAUSAGES ON A STICK LAUNCHED
BY NEW DUBLIN FIRM

Frozen sausages on a stick were launched today (6 July) by Frycicles, Ltd., a north Dublin firm owned by Dermot Dermott, the former film star. The sausages will be available throughout the country from ice-cream cabinets in grocery stores and newsagencies. They are aimed, according to Mr Dermott, at the growing number of "alternative eaters" in our society.

The questions are answered in this way:

What	Frozen Sausages
Why	"Alternative Eaters"
Who	Dermot Dermott
When	6 July
How	Ice-cream Cabinets, Grocers and Newsagents
Where	North Dublin

Readers or editors who have no interest whatever in frozen sausages can skip at that point and go to the sports section of the paper, confident that they have the essence of the story in their grasp.

Leads can take all sorts of different forms.

The Quotation Lead:

UNDER-SECRETARY DENIES CROOKERY ALLEGATIONS

"The suggestion that I constantly stole teacups, stationery and hospitality room liquor from the Houses of Parliament is totally untrue," the Under-Secretary for Belligerence today (7 July) told the Under-Secretaries' League at a routine meeting in Taunton. The Under-Secretary was responding to allegations made in the Sunday Sneer newspaper by his former secretary, Ms Ursula Vulpine. He confirmed that he had, on occasion, taken rubber bands and paperclips, but stated that this was acceptable under Parliamentary By-Laws.

Another way to do the quotation lead is this:

OLDER PEOPLE DESPISED BY YOUTH

—SOAP STAR

"In the past, women and black people were discriminated against. Today, the group most discriminated against are the over-sixties." So says Jane Gartner, the sixty year old star of "And So It Goes," the prime time soap opera currently riding high in the viewing ratings. Ms Gartner, who lives in Los Angeles, was speaking in Cork yesterday (8 July) as the guest of Growing Grey and Proud of It, a group committed to the abolition of discrimination against older citizens.

The Question Lead:

WHY ARE "WRINKLIES" HATED?

SOAP STAR ASKS

Why should older people be despised by TV comics, ignored as models in fashion photographs and commercials and brutalised by "granny bashers"?

That is the central question to be addressed by the first AGM of Growing Grey and Proud of It, opening tonight (8 July) in Jury's Hotel, Cork. The AGM, which is to be addressed by TV soap opera star Jane Gartner, will examine various aspects of prejudice affecting the over sixties.

It is also possible to do a humorous lead, although journalists at the receiving end of such a release tend to nausea and rejection. But if humour will serve to make an otherwise forgettable topic memorable or impelling, get in there and make with the jokes, witticisms and tall tales.

The first page of a press release should never be on a letter head (ordinary business notepaper). It should be on standard press release paper, or on blank white A4 paper.

Just above the headline, on the left, should be an indication to the journalist receiving it as to when it is due for release.

It may be that there is no particular secret about what you are releasing, and you are therefore giving it simultaneously to all newspapers. In which case, the underlined indication will read For Immediate Release, and the editor will be able to judge what "immediate" means by establishing the "when" in the lead paragraph.

On the other hand, it may be that you want the story to go into the Wednesday morning papers but not into the Tuesday evening ones. So you might send it out on Tuesday morning with a line reading Embargoed until 5 p.m., Tuesday 5 November 1990.

Or this kind of situation might obtain: You are releasing some information about a new kind of treatment for psoriasis. You want it to get into the *Irish Medical Times,* because the treatment will only be available to patients through their GPs, and so doctors are your primary audience. But the *Irish Medical Times,* although it appears on Thursday evening, goes to bed on Tuesday. So there is no point in releasing the thing on Thursday, because the *IMT* won't be able to take it, and because it will have appeared in several national papers by the time they get around to taking it next week, they will not give it much space. So what you do is release it on Monday, embargoed until Thursday evening, and everybody's happy. If you feel more secure, what you can do is to give it to the *Irish Medical Times* on Monday and hold all the other copies until Thursday. The *IMT* certainly are not going to run around peddling your story to other publications, and this approach eliminates the possibility of the embargo being broken deliberately or accidentally by some other publication.

Having got your dateline right, the next step is to do a good headline for your release.

One of the odd realities you have to come to terms with in this area is that the brighter your headline, the better the chance of the story making it into print—but the *lesser* the chance of the headline itself getting through untouched. For some reason, every good sub-editor is attracted by a snappy headline; and by reflex, stimulated to improve on it. When I was a fashion correspondent, I was always fascinated to see press releases coming in, accompanying beautiful pictures of new garments, and topped off with witty or provocative headlines. The subs would acknowledge the headline with a grin, put their pens through it and substitute another. Sometimes the replacement was better. Sometimes it was very much worse; witness the relentless recycling of that superannuated cliché THE LONG AND THE SHORT OF IT as a headline on fashion reports about hem-lengths.

The bottom line is that you must spend time getting a headline right, but never expect to see it atop the story as printed in your newspaper.

Getting the headline right means telling the story in a shout. That's what you're doing in any newspaper. The shout has to be gargantuan in some papers. It has been established that an average edition of the Sunday

New York Times contains more information than the average seventeenth century British village dweller encountered in his or her entire *life*. So there is a lot of competition for attention. Every headline is, in effect, a shout saying READ ME PLEASE, I AM INTERESTING.

So create a headline which:

- Tells the story in one line
- Does so with an active verb (Not "Man Bitten By Dog" but "Dog Bites Man".)
- Uses no jargon
- Is in the present or future tense if possible.

Do not put the dateline and the headline too far up on the first page. The sub-editor is likely to need to scribble all sorts of typesetting instructions on the blank bit, and therefore *needs* a blank bit. In addition, the sub who decides he or she cannot live with your headline needs space in which to scribble a creative alternative.

The dateline, the headline and the lead paragraph may be all you need on the first page of a press release, assuming you have to go to two pages. Stay on one page if you can, but not if the end result is a page crammed with single spaced typing which runs almost off the end of the paper.

FOR IMMEDIATE RELEASE

FROZEN SAUSAGES ON A STICK LAUNCHED
BY NEW DUBLIN FIRM

Frozen sausages on a stick were launched today (6 July) by Frycicles, Ltd., a north Dublin firm owned by Dermot Dermott, the former film star. The sausages will be available throughout the country from ice-cream cabinets in grocery stores and newsagencies. They are aimed, according to Mr Dermott, at the growing number of "alternative eaters" in our society.

"It is clear, from the recent success of Lebanese and Korean restaurents in this country, that there is a growing market for unusual fast foods," Mr Dermott says. "Frozen sausages on a stick may strike many people as a contradiction in terms, but in fact the savoury flavour is enhanced by the freezing process, and the end result is a particularly tasty savoury snack for a hot day."

M/F

Never carry a sentence from one page of a press release onto the next page. Finish a sentence, and indeed a paragraph, on the page where you started it, leave a decent bit of white paper, and put a mark (M/F or MORE) which indicates that you're not finished.

SAUSAGES 2

The new sausage snacks have been tested extensively in spot-market checks at home and abroad and have met with a positive consumer response, according to their inventor. They are to be manufactured to EC food standards in a converted ice cream factory in Blanchardstown, Dublin, and will be distributed by Lick and Promise, the chilled snack specialists. Sales in the first year are expected to top 700,000 units, with export markets being reached in year two of Frycicle's operation.

Dermot Dermott has spent the last fourteen years in Hollywood, starring in a series of comedies about the life and times of a pizza-maker. He confesses that when he decided to come back to his home town, he gave serious thought to setting up a pizza parlour or takeaway.

"On the return journey, however, I came across the frozen sausage idea when my plane was forced, by engine trouble, to land in Gander," he says. "It was a very fruitful diversion for me. I tasted the product, liked it, got the address of the franchise holder, and within weeks of coming home had the operation up and running."

ENDS

Further information from

Dermot Dermott (01) 111111

On the top of your second page, put a word which identifies the story and the number of the page. In the case of the Frycicles story, it would be Sausages 2.

Then you can do the rest of the paragraphs in your story, presenting the information in the form you hope it will take if it gets into tomorrow's newspaper.

No press release should ever go out without a contact name attached to it. Nor should an unreachable contact be tagged onto the end of it. Lest you think I jest, let me tell you that on one occasion, when I was on a news desk, a release on a matter of fairly major general concern came in late on a Friday afternoon.

"Ring him," the editor said, flinging the release at me. "Him" was the contact named at the end of the release. I rang. No answer. I kept ringing. At about eight that evening, I got an answer; a most civil and helpful cleaning lady who told me that the sender of the release was, as we conversed, half-way across an Alp on his way to his sring skiing holiday.

"Didn't he leave anyone in his place?" I asked desperately.

"No, I don't think so," she said tranquilly. "He really worked very hard this afternoon clearing his desk, you know how it is?"

I did. He had cleared his desk, garbage-fashion, and let the dust fall where it might. What appeared in Saturday's paper may have got him fired, because in the absence of any comment from his corporate headquarters, we could only carry reaction from groups who effectively constituted the opposition, and so his press release served as a Zip firelighter to sustain a bright, brief little blaze under his corporate ass.

Whenever you send a press release, keep a copy. More to the point, keep a copy beside your telephone so that if a journalist rings you for clarification, you don't end up guessing what you said in paragraph 4.

Developing a press list takes time. In my experience, short cuts such as the use of a press directory are counter-productive, because in the length of time it takes to get a directory into print, it goes out of date. Ring each major newspaper and find out who is the news editor, who the features editor, who the sports editor, and so on. If you want something on the front page, then you send it to the news editor. If you want it in the lengthy articles in the middle pages, you send it to the features editor. Travel editors, health editors, property editors, financial editors, economics editors, arts editors and sports editors may all be the right people to receive particular releases.

Here are some of the people who should receive press releases (or press kits or both—see the next section), depending on the kind of story you are plugging.

Release	Mail to
New cosmetic to cover birthmarks	News editors
	Features editors Art editors (Pics)
	Woman's editors (if the paper operates this system)
	Glossy magazines
	Medical publications (They may decide it's not "serious" enough, but you lose nothing.)
	Provincial papers. Health and soft current affairs TV programmes. Radio stations (if you have a very good talker who can make an essentially visual subject come alive without pictures.)

Former Rugby International becoming MD of cutlery company	News editors Business editors Sports editors (It isn't strictly speaking relevant to them, but it's a courtesy.) Business magazines Business programmes radio and TV Provincial press and radio stations.
TV star to climb Everest for charity	News editors Art editors Features editors Columnists Chat shows, radio and TV Provincial press and radio stations
Talent contest winner to record first single in Nashville	News editors Art editors Music editors Features editors Music columnists Chat shows Provincial press Every radio show on the air

Launch of new product to repair the ozone layer	News editors Environment correspondents Business editors Soft current affairs, radio and TV Provincial press and radio Every magazine printed
Statement on management position in relation to threatened go-slow	News editors Industrial Relations correspondents Hard current affairs programmes, radio and TV (*Today, Tonight* and Myles Dungan on *Drivetime*, rather than *The Gay Byrne Show* or *Nighthawks*)
Announcement of planned protest involving the dumping of 200 tonnes of imported potatoes outside Department of Agriculture	News editors Art editors Political correspondents Hard current affairs programmes, radio and TV All provincial papers and local radio stations

Announcement of new sports sponsorship by computer manufacturer	News editors Sports editors Art editors Science and Technology editors (where applicable) Chat shows, provincial papers, local radio stations
Announcement of new political party fighting to restore Irish Language as national first language	News editors Irish language editors Irish language correspondents Radio na Gaeltachta news editors Nuacht editors *Anois* Provincial Press Local Radio stations
Statement on overseas win of major literary award by Irish novelist	News editors Arts editors Soft current affairs programmes Arts programmes (this, currently, means Mike Murphy, no matter what way you slice it!) Provincial press Local radio stations

Checklist
Every Press Release Must:

- ✓ Be on white, A4 paper. Not copy paper, and if possible not thermal paper. A dirty photocopy, which looks like a fifth cousin once removed of the original document, is never acceptable. Get twenty sharp versions which look like originals from your local copy shop.
- ✓ Be typed on one side of the paper only, with 2.5 inch margin at the top of the first page and at least 1.5 inch margin on the top of the second and following pages.
- ✓ Have margins of at least an inch, preferably more, on either side.
- ✓ Be double-spaced, with good gaps between paragraphs and all quotations indented.
- ✓ Have no carryover sentences between pages.
- ✓ Have a clear indication that there is a continuation page (MORE or M/F, meaning More Following) and an equally clear indication of where the release concludes; (ENDS).
- ✓ Carry the date of release above the headline, and carry a lively headline in bold, capitalised and underlined.
- ✓ Include the WHAT, WHY, WHERE, WHEN, HOW, and WHO in the first paragraph.
- ✓ Have all spellings, figures, names, titles and claims double-checked. (In Ireland, the best source document for titles and how to refer to people is the Institute of Public Administration *Yearbook and Diary*.)
- ✓ Be written in short, clear sentences free of jargon and unexplained technicalities.

✓ Eschew printed grovels to the client:

"The good looking Managing Director of Macho, Ltd., today said forcefully that charm was merely an accident of his personality."

(If you don't believe that PR people crawl so obviously, come up and see me sometime. I have souvenirs from the sub-editor's spike which would make you weep or laugh.)

The Negative Checklist
Your Press Release May Fail If:

✗ It is imprecise in a delicate area. If, for example, it claims that diabetics no longer need worry about sugar, but name no authorities who might support the assertion, your press release will be quickly rejected.

✗ It has no news angle. Every day, in every newspaper in the land, a press release arrives which, in essence says that the John Doe Association continues to do whatever it is the John Doe Association has been doing for the last ten years. John Doe and friends are then huffy when it doesn't appear. In a world full of news, gossip, disaster, scandal, sin, success and scientific breakthrough, John Doe Associates need to take a long hard look at themselves—*or at their public relations officer*—and get the publicity act together.

✗ Similarly, there are Opinion Formers (politicians, clergymen, heads of state-sponsored bodies, CEOs and others) who generate press releases all of the time, fearlessly stating the obvious: "We are at a crossroads," they state, "and if we do not pull up our socks, we will slide rapidly downhill. Now is the time for a concerted effort to achieve national objectives, given the challenging times which lie ahead." Oh, snore, snore.

✘ It is sent to the wrong person. In a paper I worked for, one News editor was still getting releases personally addressed to him, ten years after he had retired and three years after he had snuffed it. It drove berserk the man who had succeeded him, who understandably made it policy to tear up, unopened, any envelope bearing the dead man's name.

"If they can't get *that* basic fact right, there's going to be no shagging news in it," was his judgement.

Anyone sending material to newspapers or radio stations should be doubly paranoid about checking what goes into the envelope or down the maw of the FAX machine.

Not so long ago, two highly confidential pages from a different document were inadvertently included by a commercial firm in a press release going to a national newspaper. It says volumes for the level of attention normally paid to routine releases that this particular offering was in the dustbin, together with its accidental enclosure, when a panicky press relations person rang up to find out if the newspaper had come upon it. Their interest whetted, the reporters did instant archaeology on the waste paper baskets and the two accidental pages duly made several column inches the next day. The original release went on a second journey into the waste paper basket.

✘ It is late for the publication's deadline. If, for example, you are sending something for the Christmas edition of a woman's weekly magazine, you may send it in the first week of December. The first week of December is a *whole month* too late for most glossies, which have a lead time of up to two months, and at Christmas may extend that lead time in order to do justice to the Yuletide copy.

In much the same way, if you send something to a provincial newspaper on a Wednesday so it is on the editor's desk on Thursday, it is likely to find itself accompanied on his desk by the wet-from-the-presses early copy of that particular newspaper. The danger here is that a press release, given storage, curiously becomes devalued. An editor who likes the look of it on Thursday will have gone off it by next Monday.

✘ It is a vast, self-indulgent literary essay, or a committee effort in which every fresh simplicity has been replaced by a leaden cliché or a safe vacuity.

✘ It reverses slowly to its main point. It puts everything in context before it says hello, and it modifies every statement in advance of articulating it. Having read it, the reader doesn't know whether today is Christmas or Tuesday—and doesn't much care.

✘ It has misspellings or other indications of a less than professional approach.

7

How to Assemble a Press Kit

A PRESS release says "Come here till I tell you—"

A press kit covers all angles. It may be used at press receptions where a release, on its own, might look a little bare.

It may also be used to meet the needs of special correspondents.

Thus, while a general press release about a proposed new inner city development is fine for the news desks, the Environment or Property correspondents will want much more detail about the planned buildings, photographs of the model or sketches of how the artist would see the finished development, photographs and biographical notes on the key figures in the development company, ordnance survey type maps showing precisely which area is in question, and financial data which may be too detailed for inclusion in the news release. This information should be supplied in folders, as the material from Volvo below demonstrates.

You've bought your folders; now let's work out what you're going to put into them. The options include:

The Press Release

You have a press party to launch your new product, free samples of which are handed to visiting journalists. The Managing Director makes a short, witty speech—we hope. Those journalists present take away the press kit, which includes the press release. (See pages 102 to 121 on how to construct a good release.)

A reporter from the *Daily Swank* and the *Daily Lowbrow* attends. But no reporter arrives from the *Daily Middlebrow*. You are not worried, however, because you have separately covered this eventuality by sending press releases to the desks of all major papers.

Photographs

Photography, like PR, is something which looks deceptively simple and which consquently tempts anybody owning a device marginally more sophisticated than a black-and-white polaroid to try to do it themselves. This temptation should be resisted. Search around, find a good photographic agency that knows the PR ropes, hire them and make sure that their time is cost effectively used. In other words, have your people in position, clean, sober and polished at the time the photographer is due to do his or her stuff.

Once you have had the photographs taken, you need to provide a variety of prints for different papers. If, say, you have three daily papers and a number of provincials, then what you need are exclusives for each of the national papers, and a few variants for the provincials. Thus the *Daily Swank* would get a picture of the toddler running along the beach, the *Daily Lowbrow* would get the shot of the kid falling on the sand, and the *Daily Middlebrow* the angle of the father picking the child up. Then the provincial papers would get the prints of the father marching along, carrying his son on his shoulder.

The pictures should be sharply black and white and measure either eight by six inches or eight by ten.

Great Self-Publicist: Jack the Ripper

Not only did the murderer terrorise the back streets of Victorian England, but he did it in a way that attracted maximum publicity, at the time and ever since. The bizarre details of murders, the notes written to the police and the graffiti scribbled on walls all attracted and held press attention.

From hell
Mr Lusk
Sir
I send you half the
Kidne I took from one woman
prasarved it for you tother piece I
fried and ate it was very nise. I
may send you the bloody knif that
took it out if you only wate a whil
longer
Signed Catch me when
you can
Mister Lusk

Other Visuals

There are lots of other kinds of illustrations it may be appropriate to include in a press kit.

- A press kit announcing plans for a new shopping mall or business campus must include maps, artist's impressions in reproduceable form, and photographs of the key people. It may also include photographs of a model of the development.
- A press kit to accompany a new product launch may need photographs of the packaging, in addition to pictures of the key people involved.
- A press kit to announce achievements by an industry umbrella group may need graphs and pie-charts to illustrate progress or complexity.
- A press kit to launch a new process or technology may need a graphic to give a lay person an understanding of that process of technology.
- A press kit to launch new stamps issued by AN POST would include designs for stamps. (See right)

All of these illustrations should be created in such a way as to permit reproduction. In including them in a press kit, the objective is not to entertain the journalist or to clarify things for him or her. The objective is to get the illustration in the public eye.

Try to ensure variety. There is always a danger that the creation of one truly stunning visual will lead to a situation where the *Daily Swank*, the *Daily Lowbrow* and the *Daily Middlebrow* all get shirty because no single one of them has an exclusive, and so none of them end up using your material.

Biographical Notes

If you have a visiting expert, or someone giving your product a testimonial, then biographical notes on that person must be included in your press kit.

A TV star or someone of that ilk is likely to have a biographical note already crafted and ready to photocopy. If your expert comes to you bereft of such a self-justifying note, then you have to do the research and present it yourself. Unlike a journalist, you are not seeking to achieve a warts-and-all profile. You are seeking to present a uniformly positive sequence of a man's progress to the wonderful point he now occupies. So you want a certain amount of chronology:

Born where?

Background?

Educated where?

Which degrees?

What work experience?

Published what?

Became a member of which august body when?

Travelled to where representing whom?

The best or most noted what?

Awarded which honour?

If you can also put in a couple of paragraphs indicating that this visiting fireman or woman has strong views on X, a habit of Y, and a minor obsession with Z, the chances are that you will make the person somewhat more interesting for journalists who might be persuaded to profile or interview him or her.

Once you have written the biographical note—and do try to keep it on one page—FAX it to the subject before you consider it finalised. There is nothing that more squarely damages a press reception than the celebrity guest fighting with the PR woman about an inaccurate sentence in the biographical note.

Leaflets, Booklets

Example: a company which sells peanuts has decided that eating peanuts straight from the bag is a gross under-utilisation of their marvellous potential.

So they have a press party, where they present pasta dishes and ice creams and soups and salads, all be-crisped with peanuts.

At that press party, there is a press kit which contains pictures of the various dishes, a press release and a booklet containing all of the recipes and an introduction by the television personality who is putting her reputation at stake, because she has invented the recipes.

If a book is being launched, then it depends on the price of the book and the meanness of the publisher whether or not a copy will be included in the press kit. If the book is very expensive and the publisher penurious, a pull of the cover may be included, rather than the complete book.

Samples

Example: A company is launching a series of "stocking stuffer" Christmas gifts. Small, inexpensive items like miniature staplers, leather holders for credit cards, pens that tell the time. A boxed sample of any of these will not grossly distort the shape of the folder.

Stickers

Example: a promotion for unleaded petrol may be helped by stickers for people to place in the rear window of their cars as a reminder to others.

8

Thinking in Pictures

THERE is only one thing more irritating than a cliché, and that's a true cliché.

So let's get it off our collective pectorals at this stage.

A picture is worth a thousand words

Not always, of course. If your company suddenly goes down the tubes and you owe a fortune to small suppliers, big multinationals, friends, neighbours and the Revenue Commissioners, then a fetching photograph of you in the newspaper, dimpling under an umbrella, your lashes irridescent with rain will not only not solve the problem, but will create a desire in your creditors to dimple you permanently.

In general, in the western world, we are increasingly addicted to pictures and impressions. One of the reasons is the pre-eminence of television among the informing media. More than ten years ago, in America's *Journal of Communications*, Professor George Gerbner defined the steadily growing trend.

"Television," he said, "tells most of the stories to most of the people, most of the time."

Television tells the stories, and it does it in pictures. Examining how the media handled the Reagan years, Mark Herstgaard (*On Bended Knee, The Press and the Reagan Presidency*, NY 1988) suggests that one of the central lessons the Reagan media managers learned early was "a simple truism about television: the eye always predominates over the ear when there is a fundamental clash between the two."

So, whenever there was a stink story ready to break, the media managers got their manipulative little heads together and worked out happy pictures. If, say, a depressing set of statistics was about to emerge showing that new housing projects were way down on those of the previous year, then they would fly the President to some exceptional city where new housing projects had increased, and set him down among construction workers covered in hard hats and smiles. Josh, banter and man-of-the-people charm would happen ever so naturally for the cameras, and back to the network headquarters would go footage that positively glowed in the dark with warmth and happiness. The commentator would then do a savage voice-over that spread mistrust and derision as thickly as America's flaccid libel laws would allow. But it never added up to the end result for which the editor might have hoped. Viewers viewed. Viewers gained an impression. Viewers retained that impression.

You want my personal opinion, it is that this is why TV is leading us into new, semi-literate, pervasively banal dark ages. But television, like the poor, is always with us, these days, and, realistically, if you want publicity, you probably want it on television. Whether you seek publicity for a product, a service, an idea or a personality, television—if you can interest the programmers in the story—will deliver your sales pitch to more people than will any other medium. Similarly, if you are protesting against something, television coverage of your protest will spread the awareness nationwide.

To get something on television, you have to think in pictures. This is tedious because, in addition to content, you have to have a visual element in your story. On the other hand, once you have done your visual thinking for television, the chances are that you are well on your way to interesting the Art editors of the newspapers. (The Art editor is the one who picks the pictures to go along with various reports and who bosses the photographers around.)

Now, put yourself briefly behind the Art editor's desk. The Art editor's job is to contribute heavily to the visual appeal of the newspaper by the selection of pictures. That task has to be done within certain limitations:

- Every national newspaper, every day, has to carry wire pictures of overseas disasters, space launches, riots or wars.
- On the international news pages are standard pictures of world leaders.
- On the business and news pages have to go head-and-shoulder shots of business people and politicians.

All of these are easily foretold and provide a certain comfort zone for an Art editor. After that comfort zone is established, the Art editor, ideally, would like one picture for each main section of the paper—front page, home news, leader page, feature section, business section, property/agriculture/science and technology sections—which makes passersby halt and look at a pile of evening papers on a rough wooden box in the street; a picture that grabs the eye.

> *Michael Jackson's picture perfect and wants to stay that way. So, if you have to take his picture, you'd better be ready to follow some very specific instructions. Two days before one press conference, the public relations firm for a company involved in a commercial link-up with MJ called newspapers to tell them how to prepare for the event. They not only advised photographers what size lens to put on their cameras, byt also how many feet they would be from the Gloved One and what f-stop settings to use on their camera too.*

A picture may be eye-grabbing because:

- ❑ It has someone famous in it. Try Princess Di, Elizabeth Taylor (still), Jacqueline Onassis (still) Flo Jo, Paul Hogan, Mike Tyson or Joan Collins.
- ❑ It has human horror in it: someone committing suicide by leaping from a forty storey building or a fire victim being hauled amid billowing smoke out of a window onto a ladder, or a plane in spectacular bits all over a river.
- ❑ It has pathos: a child rescued from a well after a week.
- ❑ It is funny. A famous serious person doing something unexpected can be very funny. (If the unexpected thing was unexpected and sore, the participant may not be helpless with laughter or madly keen to see the incident preserved for life in a picture, but the rest of the newspaper-buying public may still think it's a hoot.)
- ❑ It is dramatic. Unexpected. Has an angle. When you are planning the picture angle of your story, therefore, you need to work hard so that the photograph provided by you or taken by the newspaper's photographer gives the Art editor one of the list of advantages covered above.

What no Art editor *ever* wants is predictable visual tedium like:

- ✘ An earnest politician standing behind a terrified computer operator, both of them looking meaningfully at a VDU.
- ✘ A group of people standing together and pretending to read a report.
- ✘ A person having the operations of a factory described to him/her.
- ✘ A person receiving from another person an

outsized cheque.

So how can you tell your story in visual terms?

☑ Example

Cartoonist Flann O'Riain will not pay his television licence fee because there are not enough Irish language programmes to satisfy him.

Told, just like that, even if he gets taken to court and fined, the story is worth about a half an inch in the newspapers. So O'Riain (his drawings are signed *Doll*) takes his television, loads it onto a trolley, and happens to have a few photographers around as he humps it up the steps of the Department of Communications to give it to the Minister, on the basis that, without enough Irish programmes, it is worthless to its owner.

The picture duly appears, regardless of the fact that the Minister probably was not even in the building at the time, and, even if he *had* been, would never have taken O'Riain's television from him. The set remains there and O'Riain will reclaim it only when he thinks there is enough broadcasting in Irish.

☑ Example

An environmental group want to draw attention to the probability that a city will be plagued by smog in the coming winter season.

They may have all of the technical data.They may have the charts of the city, indicating where most coal fires are used as the main form of heating in cold months. They may have technicalities about the constituent elements in smoke and smog. They may have extracts from EC Directives on this topic. But if they want to get on the front pages, they will need a visual way of telling the story.

The environmental group go away and invest in dark clothes and gas masks. They get a banner made with a good slogan on it.

They notify the papers, and they head down to the main bridge, clear the middle of it, line up their three gas masked people and unfurl their banner. The picture duly appears, and, the first time, makes its point neatly. (On later re-runs, the gas mask has become a somewhat tedious motif in environmental consciousness-raising. Once you've seen one gas mask, you've seen 'em all.)

☑ Example

The people promoting Age and Opportunity are eager to establish, through the media, an awareness that being over sixty does not mean you are in a wheelchair or rocking chair for the rest of your life.

The editors and programme-makers are sympathetic, but putting words around the concept is not enough. What is needed is a picture which sums the whole thing up. What is decidedly *not* needed is a picture of an old folks" outing.

Some bright spark goes to the other end of the problem.

"Look, what are the most glamorous and active things you see people doing?" she asks.

Wild suggestions ensue, including winning gold medals at the Olympic Games. One timid soul ventures that air hostesses are a touch glamorous and not given to sloth.

"*Air hostesses*," the bright spark says thoughtfully. "Hmmmm."

Two days later, she has found a seventy-seven year old whose dream in life has always been to be an air hostess. She has also found an airline willing to allow her to be an air hostess for the day. They train and dress her. The flight takes off.

She hands out sweets from a little basket and coffee from a trolley, and poses equably for the photographers.

She comes up smiling in newspaper after newspaper the following day, establishing as no words could establish how the constraints of age can be minimised.

When you're thinking visually, you can be as creative as you want, but remember that an excuse for a picture which has no real connection to the story is likely to be seen as a gimmick. Remember, too, that the human beings involved have rights. Do not line up pictures that require someone to hold a cat, feed a baby or climb up the neck of a giraffe unless you have briefed the victim and got his or her enthusiastic consent. Nor does it have to be as exigent as giraffe-climbing. I once set up a photograph involving a man sitting, shirt-sleeves rolled up, working through papers. Compared to ascension on a giraffe, this may seem dead easy, but the subject of the picture would not do it.

"I have never taken off my jacket during a working day," he said firmly.

"Oh, come *on*," I said. "When you're very busy..."

"I never take off my jacket," he repeated. "Ever."

I looked at him, sceptical to the point of calling him a liar.

"Ask the people who work with me," he suggested.

There was a moment's pause.

"Ask my wife," he further offered.

The picture had to be changed. Another method had to be found of establishing visually that here was a man working under enormous pressure. It was done. But checking the shirt-sleeves angle with him first would have saved a lot of angst.

It's also important, when thinking about pictures, that you do not create a visual motif which is difficult to live down in future. The classic example of this, from the early days of 'sixties feminism, was when one group, *once*, burned a handful of bras as a way of rejecting over-emphasis on female vital statistics.

It may have provided a useful picture at the time,

but it hung a weight around feminism which grew more and more tiresome as decades passed, and cries of "Oh, you're a bra-burner, are you?" punctuated discussions on human rights.

Now, let's move away from cleverly designed "photo opportunities" and into the occasional need for more formal photographs.

Can you take them yourself?

If you have the equipment, the time, the training, the instinct, the patience and the professionalism, the answer is "yes". Years ago, as a struggling young journalist working as a "stringer" for an English newspaper, I realised I could double the pittance I was earning if I supplied the pictures as well as the words. Borrowing my boyfriend's good Olympus camera, I got ten minutes-worth of instruction from him on how to get sharp pictures and judge depth of field, and, with the courage of my ignorance, started to take pictures. Lichfield I wasn't, but the pictures printed up well, money passed hands and I figured the best thing was to marry the boyfriend, because then what was his would be mine too, including the camera. Fourteen years later, it is still functioning and has been used for all sorts of publicity and other pictures.

None of which adds up to an endorsement of amateur photography rather than professional photography. If your friendly local amateur shutter-clicker produces poor quality pictures cheaply but at a considerable cost in time, then shoot him in the lens and go to the professionals.

For portraits, it's worth noting that:

✓ Glasses need to be shot with particular care, because of reflected light.

✓ Fat people should wear dark clothing if they want to look thinner.

✓ Irrelevant badges should be kept off lapels.

Communication with a photographer has to be a two-way thing.

You need to be very clear what you want to achieve, and brief the photographer accordingly. Contrariwise, you should listen to any suggestions the photographer may have.

When my company was having a few pictures taken of our video production unit in action, the photographer suggested that, for some of the shots, one of our marked vehicles be put in the background. Someone drove the car into position, the shot was committed to film, and the advice was forgotten. Until the picture subsequently appeared, without a caption identifying it as being from Carr Communications, in a newspaper feature about video production. The words along the side of the car left readers in no doubt as to where the crew shooting the video were from.

Final thought

This comes under the Last But Not Least heading. A picture without a caption is a dead loss to a newspaper. The caption should say what's in the picture:

> Joe Bloggs, Chief Executive of the Fly By Night Association, Jane Doe, Director of the Hardly Ables League, and Ann Other, representing the Innocent Bystander Brigade, pictured at today's launch of the *Loony Tunes* free cartoon sheet. The new cartoon sheets will be available to under-tens at street corners from next Thursday (10 August).
>
> Further information from:
>
> Anita Bloggs (01) 111111

9

Staging a Reception, Press Conference or Seminar

If you want to reach the media *en masse,* as opposed to getting cosily informative with one journalist or broadcaster, you may feel the need to hold a reception, run a press conference or stage a seminar.

The differences between the three go like this:

A Reception

This is an informal event, a little like a cocktail party, with drinks, canapés, free samples of something to take away, and the briefest of pleasant speeches. Receptions make most sense if you want to launch something which is soft, rather than hard news. Publicity for books being published often centre on a reception in the early evening. If you are releasing a new bubble bath, instant house plant or self-draping wallpaper, then a reception may be the most cost- effective way to bring the good news to the widest number of journalists. They must go away with samples of the product in containers which do not embarrass them; I remember a small mutiny breaking out, years ago, when a number of feature writers, myself included, attended the launch of a wallpaper, only to be handed, at departure time, carrier bags out of which poked six rolls of wall covering. The first journalist to receive this unexpected gift was stricken with sudden silence in the face of conflicting reactions. She was quite taken with the idea of decorating her new offspring's room free of cost, appalled by the panicked peony pink of the rolls and flummoxed by the aggregate weight. Dumbly, she headed out of the reception room and, with some difficulty, reached the head of the stairs, at which point the carrier bag suffered plastic fatigue and disgorged the rolls in a disorderly tumult down towards the next floor of the hotel, where they attacked two passing waiters and flailed them about the shins. Watching this, the rest of the journalists lost interest in the wallpaper-transport business and stalked out.

If you're planning a reception, much of the advice which follows, related to invitations, phone-arounds, and press kits, is relevant. The exception is that if it's a fairly frivolous product you are launching, and if you are launching it at an appropriate time, then a facetious or off-beat invitation is acceptable. One book publicist invited journalists to a reception to launch a book about cocktails by enclosing a shrink-wrapped martini.

Coming up to Christmas one year, a PR pal of mine sent an invitation to journalists which had batteries taped to it, and a funny tag line to suggest a) that the journalists use them to power their progress to the reception, and b) that the toy being launched at the reception would run for two whole days on these four little batteries. The safest rule about light touches related to invitations is; if in doubt, don't. A gimmick gone off the boil does nobody any good.

Invitations to "soft news" receptions should go particularly to Art editors (assuming that you can generate good ideas for pictures), to feature writers, columnists and diarists.

A Press Conference

This is what you call when you have good hard news about something people are interested in. Hard news is something different; the results of a study or survey, an attack by someone eminent on a particular way of doing things , the release of designs for a new town, the appointment of a new board, the confession of dreadful results or the statement of a massive donation to a charity.

A press conference can be at any time of the day, but is arguably best just before lunchtime. This timing means that if the journalists have the time, they can stay for lunch. It also means that evening paper writers can get a fast summary of the story to their editors before the paper is printed, but that the daily newspaper journalists have more detailed information for the following morning's editions.

Invitations to press conferences should be informative and non-facetious. Printed, embossed cards dipped in gold leaf are neither necessary nor desirable: a brief note on a business letter head, which gives all of the relevant facts, is simple and functional. (See below)

They should go to News editors and thereafter to all of the journalists to whom you might send an invitation to a reception. (See pages 114 to 117).

The Chairman and Directors of Bloggs PLC
invite you to attend a Press Conference

In: Fitzwilliam Suite, Anna Livia Hotel,
Dublin 2
On: Tuesday July 17th
At: 12 noon

when details of the company's latest
acquisition will be announced

For further information
Tom Smith
Tel: 01/111111 (office)
01/111111 (home)

Somewhere between seventy and a hundred invitations may go out to a wide variety of journalists, including freelances, to arrive one week in advance of the press conference. On the day after the invitations should have slapped down on the journalists' desks, the phone calls start. The first call goes something like this:

PR Person:	"Howya, Jo. Aideen here."
Journalist:	"Aideen? Oh. Yeah. Hi."
PR Person:	"Did you get an invite from me? I sent it yesterday..."
Journalist:	"To the Whistle-Blowers' Law thing? Yes. Have it here in front of me."
PR Person:	"Great. Just checking. Thanks."

The second call happens on the day before the press conference or on the morning of the day it is being held. That call is to check who actually has a firm intention of going to the event.

For every invitation which results in a firm intention to attend there are eight or nine which do not. So out of seventy invitations, you may reasonably expect six or seven attenders. If the wind is in the right direction, there may be more. If the gods have turned their faces away, there may be fewer.

Having made the calls to the people who agree to come, you may also make phone calls to the people who will not go to the reception or press conference, but who are eager to have the information dispensed

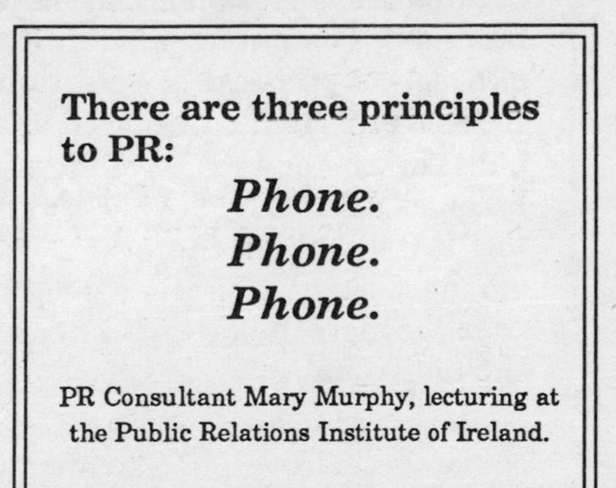

to them over the wires.

Phone calls are part of a complex of activities which need to happen before the press conference. One of the first things to be done is the selection of a venue. You select a venue firstly because of location: city centre, rather than outlying area, no matter how picturesque the latter may be. Journalists have a limited time and they prefer hostelries which are around the corner from their offices. The second factor in venue selection is size. Based on the number of people you expect to be there, as opposed to the number of invitations sent out, you pick a room of the right size. Too large a room makes your event look as if only a handful of people arrived. Too small a room means that nobody can move, drink or write notes. If in doubt, err on the side of largeness, because a large room can be broken into segments of more manageable scope by the use of screens or accordion-pleated barriers. Always keep in mind that the journalists attending a press conference are only part of the story; lots of people from the company involved will want to attend, too.

Traditionally, at the entrance to the room is placed a table, manned or womanned by a welcoming person, and equipped with a Visitors' Book into which guests inscribe their names and the names of the organisations or publications for which they work. This practice is beginning to fade, although it has its points as a method of checking who attended and who got side-tracked and must be followed up subsequently. Where a PR person knows most of the journalists attending, it becomes a frank irrelevance, and where a person new to PR is handling the event, the danger is that the emphasis on getting the names scribbled will distract from the more important imperative of getting to know the individual.

Backdrops can be most important for press conferences, in order to create a bright background to carry a logo or other identifier for the television and stills cameras to focus on. This provides an instant visual reminder of what the event was all about. The cost of design and the make up of a backdrop run into several hundred pounds, but if the basic structure is well made, it can have later outings. A backdrop needs to be just under seven feet in height, to accommodate the tallest guest who may need to be photographed in front of it.

The speeches should be brief and to the point. You can tell your client that and make him or her live with it. The same applies if, say, a sporting personality is involved. In general, such personalities are only too happy to be civilly terse. If, however, you have a Government minister making a speech at your event, you have relatively little control over what is said or the length to which the speaker goes. In advance of the event, the relevant Private Secretary or other Department official may contact you and ask for some background material on your company or organisation. This phonecall will also ascertain details about the purpose and parameters of the particular event. Government speakers, in every country, range from those who are witty, wise and to the point to those who wander all over the shop and seem to have taken out a franchise on tedium. PR people cannot pick and choose. It is only appropriate to invite the man or woman whose portfolio relates to the topic being publicised. Even then, the chances of netting a minister are limited.

Journalists attending a press conference have different, and sometimes competing needs. A TV reporter will want to set up a brightly-lit interview with a central figure and will not want any other journalist's voice to be heard during the recording, whereas print journalists may be quite happy to muck in all at the one time. Catering for the needs of both types of reporter requires planning, decision and delicacy.

Making the most of any TV interviews that arise means preparing your client so that he or she can tightly summarise the most important aspects of the story. As I write, a radio news bulletin from a local radio station is playing on my desk, and a Managing Director is commenting from a press conference about a product which has had to be withdrawn from sale for safety reasons. The interview segment lasts twenty-three seconds. As "sound bites" go, that is long, these days. Many news bulletins on television will have newsmakers commenting for as little as eleven seconds. If the person who owns the story cannot tell it quickly, simply and vividly, then that person needs ruthless training if they're not to end up on the cutting-room floor.

As journalists leave the press conference, they should receive a press kit containing a release and any other information necessary. Under *no circumstances* should a speech be handed out before the speechmaker utters it. When this is done, what happens is that the audience can—and do—read it faster than the speaker who is articulating it, and so they have reached the funny or exciting bits before the speaker does. The release of hard-copy of speeches happens more often than is justified. Frequently, a summary or press release is what is needed.

Photographers often arrive before the journalists with whom they supposedly work. If they arrive before the speechmaking starts, facilitate their getting whatever shot they want, and make sure they have the spelling of the relevant names right. If they fail to arrive, the PR person in charge will have prevented disaster by having an agency photographer on hand to take pictures which can be given, free of charge, to the newspapers or magazines which do not send picture-takers to the event. The agency photographer should use a variety of different angles and groupings of people, so that no two publications receive precisely the same shot.

Seminars

These may last a day or longer, and will cover a number of topics within a related theme. In structuring a seminar with media coverage in mind, it is vital that a series of contrasting topics and speaker types be offered, and, if possible, that a big name be involved. Technical speakers need to be balanced against populist speakers. Let's say, for example, that you're running a National Food Handlers' Seminar. The day might go like this:

INTRODUCTION Minister for Food	With luck, he'll announce new plans to standardise the proper ingredients for killer cocktails, or something equally catchy.
KEYNOTE ADDRESS Larry A. Waterprice	Larry is a scientific genius who has developed a new syrup for the production of cough sweets, which prevents some obscure side-effect of earlier cough sweets. He did it —and will talk about doing it— by means of splitting an enzyme with an atom and adding a whatsit or two

under centrifugal force. Highly technical, but a scientific breakthrough.

SECOND SPEECH
Arnie Bentwood

Arnie is introducing new technology in food processing. Machines that use less power than before will pillage a prune, devastate an onion, or ravage rhubarb and, with an extra fitment or two, allow themselves to be used to mow lawns or play compact discs.

THIRD SPEECH
Percy Dunnit

Nutrition expert who says that whole grains, minimally attacked by a food processor and allied with a lively sex life, are the ultimate keys to good health. This is supported by a great deal of visual material which makes his copious statistics somewhat more digestible.

FINAL SPEECH
Norman Enorp

Norman is an advertising expert who feels the current legislation limiting the claims which can be made for health foods is unjust, and is prepared to say so in blunt terms.

If the appropriate material is aimed at different journalists in different media, then the end result might be along the following lines.

National TV News

Newsreader: "The Minister for Food today called for an end to imprecise alcohol measures in cocktail bars. Speaking at a seminar on food processing, he suggested to our correspondent that the current situation had gone on too long."

Minister: "Ideally, we should have a situation where a Manhattan has precisely three parts..."

The Daily Opinion Formers' Paper

Scientific breakthrough on cough therapy product

A SCIENTIFIC breakthrough announced yesterday at the National Seminar on Food Processing, will eliminate an unpleasant side effect of OTC cough preparations. Food processing professionals attending the seminar heard yesterday how a Swiss research and development laboratory had found that by splitting enzyme XH under centrifugal...

The Impulse Buyers' Popular Paper

KITCHEN GADGETS WILL GET THE DOMESTIC ACT TOGETHER

The National Seminar on Food Processing was told yesterday that kitchen gadgets will soon run the whole house.

"We'll have food processors that will mow lawns," seminar speaker Arnie Bentwood predicted, "and, with a small adjustment, they will also play compact discs."

The Truck Drivers' Tabloid

Bonking and Bran the Key to Health

A leading expert said yesterday that bonking could be regarded as a useful form of exercise. He told a seminar on food processing that whole grain foods, like bran, linked to a lively sex life, were the key to good health.

If you are structuring a complete seminar or conference, then you must try to ensure that your speakers, individually and severally, provide the audience with something which is new or different. If, on the other hand, you are just adapting your own contribution to someone *else's* conference, you must make sure that your contribution gives the journalists present the material to make a report. Think up the headline you would like before you compose your address.

A reception, a press conference and a seminar can all go wrong. Let me give you some examples culled from friends in the business.

- *"I was launching a book. New book. New writers. New everything. Plus a prestigious literary figure to make a speech. Everything in place, and no journalists. I couldn't figure out why not a single solitary scribe was turning up, and eventually I slipped away to phone one of the papers, to find that a major accident had happened. There were hundreds of dead and injured, spectacular damage to the area surrounding the accident, weeping relatives, accusations flying, ambulances whining. There was no chance that any journalist or photographer could get to my reception, so all I could do was turn it into a happy launch party for the people directly involved, and get to work immediately on all my feature writer friends to see what they would do, after the event. The coverage, after about three weeks, was respectable enough to nudge the book briefly onto the bestseller list, but it was touch and go."*

- *"What happened to my press conference was a director who couldn't keep his mouth shut. We were launching a new product and everything was looking great, except that this man didn't have anything to do, and so he got casually talking with one of the journalists. So casually did he talk that he inadvertently gave the journalist a clue that the finances of the company were in rag order and that we were threatened with the Fraud Squad at any moment. The journalist, who had been half asleep, woke up awful fast, and what had been a private problem well on its way to solution became a front page disaster. Meanwhile, it was wrist-slitting time for all the unfortunates who had developed what was a really good new product. And no possibility of a rescue..."*

■ *"It was one of those evenings you cannot prevent, even by the best planning. We were running on the same night as four other major announcements. Journalists made choices, and unfortunately most of them decided against coming to our launch. I had our people commandeer telephones and ring reporters within each of the newspapers, and the end result was coverage as good as if they had been at the reception, because we supplied great pictures."*

■ *"The people who were designing and making the backdrop did so—and then delivered it to the wrong city. With about ten minutes to go, we tracked it down and realised that there wasn't a snowball's chance in hell that it was going to arrive in time. So three of us commandeered the most astonishing array of bits of cardboard, old movie posters turned around the wrong way, brochures and leaflets, and concocted a backdrop that looked quite acceptable, if you were a bit myopic. The only problem was that it was half the height of the normal backdrop, so when the TV cameramen were working, we propped the thing on the table beside the man being interviewed.*

The reporter was awfully decent—he held the thing upright while he did the interview, and the pictures on the news that night were fine. Clients never mind hassle as long as the eventual coverage achieved is satisfactory, so we didn't lose the retainer. But the design company lost our business so fast you could see the skid marks."

Receptions, press conferences and seminars run well when the person in charge has a series of checklists, and ticks off the details relentlessly at all stages. That includes making sure the loos nearest the reception room are civilised and that the noticeboard in the lobby indicating where the event is taking place is readable and accurate. The person in charge does not eat anything containing garlic for three days before a reception or conference and eschews alcohol until the last journalist has departed the premises.

10

Doing it Right with Daffodils —A Case History

One of the best promotions in recent years was Daffodil Day.

Charles Cully, a Dublin businessman who has something of a franchise on bright ideas, spotted this one in Canada. The basic idea is that on a specially designated day daffodils are used to raise funds to allow the development of a cadre of specially-trained nurses geared to give specialised care to cancer sufferers.

Ideas Man, Charles Cully

Daffodil Day was piloted in 1988 in Ireland, and it was decided to push it in a big way the following year. Clearly, publicity was vital, both on the day, so that as many people as possible would actually buy daffodils and thereby benefit the Irish Cancer Society, and in the months leading up to the Day, so as to attract as much community and corporate involvement as possible.

So publicity had to be wall-to-wall, but it could not be *purchased* publicity. It had to be achieved without purchase of advertising space. The end result was a PR *tour de force*, orchestrated over the months leading up to March.

November

It all started in November with a bulb planting; a photocall in the Botanic Gardens with student nurses planting the pedigree bulbs.

December

Next step was to send a press release everywhere establishing exactly what had been achieved in '88, and outlining how the money would be spent. The same press release went to each provincial paper, telling what each county had contributed the year before. In December, the first nurse, funded by the previous year's activities, was appointed in Kilkenny. This was announced on the Cancer Society's premises with press release distributed everywhere and a profile in one paper of a typical day's work—visiting people in their homes.

January

Negotiations started with all ad agencies, designers, supermarkets, petrol companies, asking for free whatever it was they did, for a good cause.

The payoff was marvellous:

- Metrovision—the giant moving signs people—gave free campaigns worth over £5,000.
- Adshel gave free hoardings all over town for Daffodil Day posters.
- Maxol gave all of their in-station hoardings—more than 5,000 of them—for personality posters commissioned specially. They also offered to sell daffodils in all their stations.
- Personalities gave their time freely and willingly.
- Telecom and a number of other companies gave their own advertising space on television to slot in Daffodil Day ads.
- Late in January there was a photocall for the College of Marketing and Design who had been asked to design a backdrop for the launch—a very impressive display of giant daffodils.

February

At the beginning of February was announced the official date of Daffodil Day '89, in three separate venues—Dublin, Cork and Galway. Another announcement was of the choice of Daffodil Nurse to symbolise Daffodil Day.

Mid-February, personality posters showing Pat Kenny, Derek Davis, Ann Doyle and Bibi Baskin were hung. The personalities all gave the use of their famous faces for free, and the decision was taken that the cheaper option would be best: black-and-white posters with one bright yellow point—the daffodil each personality was pinning to the lapel of his or her jacket. Not just because of money saved; the black and white with the spark of yellow attracted much more attention than full colour pictures would have done.

Maxol organised some publicity themselves—the posters were theirs exclusively.

Because of the RTE connection the *RTE Guide* ran all four pictures in colour—and the *RTE Guide* is the magazine with the widest circulation in Ireland.

Someone had the idea that involving radio and TV soap operas with Daffodil Day might have useful payoff. So the someone with the bright idea was sent off to speak to the producers/writers of both radio's *Harbour Hotel* and TV's *Glenroe*. Would they do something? Yes, they would. But what?

The Daffodil Day people explained to the drama people that there were a number of points which had to be got across;

1. Official wrapping paper, so that every daffodil sold would earn money for the Cancer Society.
2. Need for volunteers
3. Need for contributions of daffodils on the day. The drama people agreed to write scenes around each of these. For continuity's sake, Daffodil Day also featured in the follow-up show, saying how the day had gone "last week." Daffodil Day was on a Thursday, so *Glenroe* featured it on the preceding and following Sundays.

While the programmes were being filmed a

photographer took stills of the cast with daffodils.

To continue the excitement in newspapers late in February, stories were suggested to reporters about fears of a shortage of daffodils; they were blooming too early due to the early spring. (People were not waking up at night trembling because of the prophesied shortage of daffodils, but nevertheless, it made a good story, as did the fact that Dublin Corporation was keeping an eye on the miles of country council flower beds from where vandals had stolen daffodils the previous year.

The "possible shortage of daffodils" story then gave rise to a related saga, positive this time, about the farmer in Limerick who had a method of "saving" daffodils, which involved cutting them early before they bloomed, freezing them, and on Daffodil Day, subjecting them to heat and selling them. The farmer was worthy of television coverage and reports in all papers, both from the human interest point of view and because of his own business success story: he had started from nothing just a couple of years previously. The following year, some of the stories noted, he hoped to supply Canada with flowers for *their* Daffodil Day.

One of the ways of achieving coverage in all of the provincial papers was to send them a picture with some local VIP. But where are VIPs from all over the country concentrated, and reasonably well-motivated to pose with daffodils for a charity? Leinster House, the Irish House of Parliament, of course. It's full of politicians from all over the place, who responded warmly to the idea of a photocall in Buswell's Hotel to publicise the idea of Daffodil Day. Over two days, all the politicians were photographed being presented with daffodils by the Daffodil nurse. As the politicians had the photos taken—politicians of all parties, singly and in groups—they were asked the names of their pet local papers and journalists. The subsequent success rate with placement of pictures was 100%.

March

By this time events were planned almost on a daily basis. Every company making an order for a sizeable amount of daffodils was offered the Daffodil nurse for a photocall. Lots of them—Elan, Aer Lingus, Iarnrod Eireann accepted this offer and managed to achieve their own publicity.

Not everything worked, as the organisers recall:

"We asked Aer Lingus if they would substitute the shamrock on their planes for daffodils as an angle for the Late Late Show. The Late Late were interested but could not give copper fastened guarantees. Without a guarantee, Aer Lingus viewed the cost of changing the decals, plus the cost of grounding even one plane to have the thing transferred as enormous. The idea died for television, but we got coverage in the nationals, sans pictures, for the shamrock giving way to a daffodil."

About this time, radio and television programmes began to take items for in and around the day itself. *Live at 3* agreed to take two Daffodil nurses to talk about their routine. All programmes going out live on the day—*Jo Maxi*, *Nighthawks* etc, filled their studios with flowers which were sent to them. Andy O'Mahony, Pat Kenny, Gerry Ryan, Gay Byrne all agreed to do items on the day. The priority was to find different angles for each separate programme.

Coming up to St Patrick's Day, companies offered to deck their floats out in daffodils. This happened and worked well. A photocall had already been set up with Alice Glenn, the Deputy Lord Mayor of Dublin, sitting in the Mayoral Coach outside the Mansion House, being presented with daffodils by the nurse.

Tony Gregory agreed to don a Daffodil tie (for the photocall) in advance of the day.

The next task was to seek and set up a photocall with the Taoiseach to appear the day before Daffodil Day.

All provincial papers had been sent bromides of the daffodil logo which they used instead of their usual mastheads for the issue of that week.

Events were set up around the country (for RTE news cameras) in advance of the day. RTE was sent an itinerary which they used.

The events in Dublin included:

- Conveyor belt taking daffodils onto B&I ship.
- Alan Dukes collecting daffodils from the Cancer Society and putting them in the boot of his car.
- New AN POST motorcycle couriers doing the same and zipping off around the city (they had launched the new courier service earlier in the week.)

In Limerick:

- Aer Lingus hostesses were pictured around Shannon Airport picking any spare daffodils they could find.

In the West:

- A flight was filmed taking off for the Aran Islands with daffodils.
- In Galway, an organisation planted giant daffodils, twelve feet tall, on the main road.

RTE made a lovely newstime collage out of all these events.

On Daffodil Day itself, newscaster Ann Doyle sold daffodils by the Molly Malone statue in Grafton Street—and inevitably attracted cameras as bees to honey and moths to a flame.

The *Gerry Ryan Show* sent their intrepid reporters, Barbara and Brenda, one to Galway and one to Limerick, to see who could sell the most daffodils. Armed with mobile phones, they kept in constant contact with the show and it amounted to three hours of incredibly funny on-air daffodil selling.

The campaign director and the Chief Executive of the Irish Cancer Society gave interviews on a number of radio and TV programmes.

When it was all over, the Irish Cancer Society gave wide distribution to a newsletter giving credit wherever credit was due and reinforcing the message of the promotion.

Daffodil Day is an important example for anyone seeking to achieve publicity for fundraising or similar purposes. It made marvellously creative use of a wide range of media opportunities, not in an exploitative way, but in a way which gave added value to each media outlet, whether that was a radio features programme, a provincial newspaper or a TV serial. It obviously provides an Irish example of an achievement that could be mirrored anywhere, on a smaller or a larger scale, by using similar tactics and techniques.

Daffodil Day showed, yet again, how very generous people can be, whether as individuals or as corporate groups. In its use of famous and unknown volunteers, the day at no stage lost sight of its central objective.

Above all, what Daffodil Day showed was that a subject—cancer—which tends to create fear and rejection can be handled in a realistic but up-beat way so that people face up to the fact that cancer patients may need very specialised nursing, either to recover from surgery and other therapy, or to help in terminal stages of the disease. This message underpinned all of the months of publicity leading up to Daffodil Day itself, yet the overall campaign created a sense of coping and of optimism—as well as earning hundreds of thousands of pounds for a demonstrably good cause.

11

Starting from Bad Publicity

THERE you are, minding your own business, tending your tulips and planning no evil deeds, when you get a sudden attack of bad publicity. Your business emits a toxic cloud, your partner runs off with everybody's money, someone finds nuts and bolts in your exclusive pear marmalade or a competitor spews a few telling allegations about you.

You're in the headlines, you're on the front pages, the radio news bulletins mention you, and you can feel yourself shrivelling from the heat of the spotlights.

The best advice, in this context, can be summed up by three old laws:

- Prevention is better than cure
- When you're in a hole, stop digging

  and
- Tell the truth and shame the devil

Let's start with an example of failure to take all three pieces of advice. Her name was Rosie Ruiz. She became, literally, a nine-day wonder, when she was the unexpected winner of the Boston Marathon, on April 22, 1980.

Day One saw the good news breaking.

Day Two saw a question mark going in behind that good news. A *New York Times* columnist quoted a woman who said that Ms Ruiz couldn't have won the Marathon, because another woman had seen her travelling on the subway between two of the Marathon's stages, and winning a Marathon on subway wheels seemed like over-use of technology.

By the end of Day Two, it was pretty clear that the "winner" of the race had not prevented disaster, but might have fairly actively contributed to it.

Day Three put Ms Ruiz in front of a press conference, where she talked about brain surgery in her past, swore she would not be victimised by rumours and claimed to have run the race from start to finish, *sans* subway.

Days Four, Five and Six had friends of Ms Ruiz saying "Perish the thought, she isn't the type, she wouldn't, she couldn't, she didn't and it's only wicked media making sensations." A pretty good example, this, of continuing, on your own and with help, to dig when you have found yourself in a sizeable hole.

Day Nine was when the *New York Times* announced that the Marathon Committee had stripped Rosie Ruiz of her status as winner.

On the previous days, the media had chopped their marathon cabbage in as many ways as they legitimately could. They examined the pressures on runners, editorialised on the ethics involved, and looked at famous cheats of our time. During this outbreak of print and electronic media coverage, Ms Ruiz, like Brer Rabbit, lay low and said nuthin', other than that she was being advised by lawyers. (Well, she would, wouldn't she?) She thus failed to deliver on the last of our three pieces of advice: she failed to tell the truth and shame the devil.

But, I hear you say, such an example is rare.

This is true. On the other hand, you open today's papers, and you will find that unprevented disaster of various dimensions gives rise to many of the reports therein. Bad news is always news, and prevention of disaster is the best method of preventing negative coverage.

Obviously, not all disasters can be headed off at the pass. Preventive medicine for hurricanes has yet to be invented. Market turndowns happen. If your partner is clever with the books and bereft of a moral sense, he/she may rob you blind and take off for Barbados, leaving you to face the off-key music that results.

However, a great deal of what lands people in the media soup should be prevented by "worst scenario" planning. Children do it all the time. They imagine what it would be like to have no arms or to go blind, and they act out how they would cope with such a problem. Or rather, they act it out until some adult half-wit comes along, shudders at this negative thinking, and tells them not to play such horrible games. Do they not know they could be left like that if the wind changed.

When planning the public profile of you as an individual, or the public profile of an organisation or company, it is imperative to envisage and plan for precisely what would happen *if the wind changed.*

This planning needs to be ruthlessly honest and to operate from a total faith in Murphy's Law—if something can go wrong, it will.

Curiously, the higher-tech the operation, the more reluctant to consider Murphy's Law the people become. Oh, no, they say, this plant could not have a disaster. We have so many regulations, so many cross-checks, such a concentration on quality control. The next time you meet them, they're wearing overcoats and muslin muzzles because the roof has just blown into the next county and an unidentified pong is whirling up everybody's nostrils.

Murphy's Law rules, OK? OK.

So, if you're running a business which involves any hazardous or highly inflammable materials, you imagine the worst that could happen and plan accordingly. The larger companies tend to have emergency communications plans not only in their systems, but tested in the same way you would test a fire drill. So a company with an offshore oil rig has a communications drill ready to go into action should something happen on that oil rig. People on the rig have a number of priority messages to transmit. Based on those messages, or lack of them, the people on shore have identified tasks. One may have to contact the police, the fire brigade and the local authorities. One may have to contact the relatives of those on the rig, to reach them before the news bulletins create panic. One may have to contact the key media. But that's only first base. From then on, more detailed information is needed by media, who want to know (remember Kipling's six serving men):

What happened?

Where?

To **who(m)**?

Why?

When?

What's going on now?

An emergency communications plan should seek to meet the needs of a number of different publics, and should place a high priority on relatives of those who may be injured by an accident, and an equal priority on community concern about, say, environmental hazard. It should also keep the interests of the company to the forefront; so if it is not of major public concern that a £500,000 computer got burned to a crisp, it may not be in the interests of the company to announce this immolation, since that may immediately call in question the future of the company, alert debtors to shrug and postpone payment and stimulate creditors to come knocking on the singed front door yelling for money.

When planning emergency communications materials—like press releases—it is imperative that the structure be in place, preferably on a word processor, and that the structure is clear of all irrelevancies. If a tsunami has just washed your business into the North Sea, then a press release stuffed with details about how your CEO got a Grammy Award in his previous job is not the most useful thing as far as the press is concerned. By all means, have a fact sheet to hand which indicates what the company is, what it does, where it markets, what its successes have been, what brands are associated with it, and who are the guiding lights within the corporate hierarchy, but do not shove all of this into a press release.

All "worst scenario" planning should assume a Woodward and Bernstein-like enthusiasm for muckraking among the journalistic community, and should be prepared for the most negative questions. Muckraking is an essential component of good journalism (see Jessica Mitford's *Confessions of a Muckraker*) and is often triggered by bad news. Random, inexplicable calamity is profoundly threatening, and attribution of responsibility tends to mitigate that threat. Hence the public wants someone to blame for a disaster and the journalist wants to find someone guilty of something.

If you are a bird alone, that is of enormous help when disaster strikes, because you will be singing a singular song. A group, organisation or company can have a considerable problem in the same situation, in that too many may start singing simultaneously, and they may not be singing the same song. There should be an agreed communications path, and it should not necessarily start with the PR person or, worse still, the PR agency. If, out of the blue, you have three million pounds that's slightly missing, then the financial journalists do not want your PR agency running around the place spewing shiny generalities about pursuit of excellence. They want to talk to the man in charge or the woman in charge right now, please. And they want to do it without a PR person standing at the elbow of the person in charge, editing the output as it outputs. If the CEO is not available to give the straight dope, then a deputy will do. Or a specialist; in the event of financial disaster, the Financial Controller becomes relevant, whereas if there is a strike, the Personnel Manager can be useful. Media prefers to have a horse's mouth who can be named, rather than a PR person or an anonymous spokesperson.

Remember, too, that "worst scenario" planning should not start with the headlines. It should start with the realities.

Assuming you cannot prevent disaster, can you control disaster when it happens? Are all of your people clear on emergency procedures? If contamination hits your product, have you a plan for pulling it from the shelves? In regard to the latter, the Tylenol people provided an object lesson in how to cope when hit by the most bizarre disaster when a psychopath poisoned some of their capsules, and brought about several deaths. The product was pulled, information was provided and a replacement product quickly developed, so that within a startlingly short time, *caplets,* which are less easily tinkered with, were available in drug stores and pharmacies. Not only did the company cope well with the disaster, but their coping created positive publicity, as mentioned on page 98.

The second of the three old saws is "When you're in a hole, stop digging." When bad news hits the headlines, undirected panicky activity may be the worst thing you can do. Count to a hundred before you even *think* of uttering, and then count to a thousand.

The urge to contradict, refute, hold a press conference or attack an opponent may all translate into a needless prolongation of the disaster, where discretion, damage limitation or just plain silence would help the thing to die down.

A couple of years ago a company asked me to examine what had happened to them after they had had several months of bad publicity, and tell them why the public regarded them as muck. A quick read through their cuttings provided Exhibit A and Exhibit B.

Exhibit A was a report in an evening newspaper which suggested that the company did not have the highest standards in their business. The report ran on page 4, and the reference, which came at the end of a story on something quite different, measured one and a half inches.

Exhibit B was the press statement the company issued in response. It did a number of things, none of them beneficial to the company:

- ✘ It elaborated the brief reference in the evening paper, so that instead of a vague, non-specific, unmemorably woolly accusation, what was presented was a detailed, vivid and memorable version of the same thing.
- ✘ It was pompous, huffy and defensive in tone.
- ✘ It left a number of loose ends hanging, so that instead of sealing off the stinker, it opened wonderful extension possibilities.
- ✘ Because it was released to all media, it created a window of visibility which the original story had not had. Evening papers are not read as thoroughly or as widely as are daily papers. The response and reiteration of the problem was given space in all of the national morning papers and on radio. It amounted to megaphone crying

over a teaspoonful of spilt milk.

When this was explained to the Managing Director, he shouted (while I listened) at his PRO, demanding that the PRO justify having got them into such a comprehensive stew.

The PRO shouted back.

"You told me to *do* something," he pointed out. "You wanted it done *immediately*. You wanted the problem *fixed*. You didn't call for silence. You wanted headlines proclaiming our innocence."

"I didn't want headlines full of words like "defends" and "claims'," the MD bellowed.

"If someone says you're in the wrong, and you say no I'm not, what the hell else is the newspaper going to say except that you're defending yourself?"

There was a long silence.

"They could say we refuted," the MD said weakly.

"Refuted!" the PRO spluttered, making it sound like a weak dirty word. "Refuted!"

It was left to me to point out to the MD that the press release had been an example of someone in a hole continuing to dig vigorously, and that if a solicitor's letter had gone to the person who accused them, in the wrong, it would have warned that detractor to keep his beak buttoned, lest he find himself in court. "But there was always the chance the morning papers would have picked it up anyway," the PRO said, becoming retrospectively enamoured of his incendiary press release. "One of them might have," I agreed. I did not add what I felt, which was that all of them were unlikely to. Nor did I suggest that the one which did pick it up could have been given a correction, not enough added value to fill a large volume.

When a media problem arises, it is important that

the person or company or organisation on the sharp edge does not start in the transmission mode, but in the analysis mode. If there is a likelihood that someone will sue somebody else, then a legal adviser should be in on the discussion. Above all, the natural desire to communicate, and the even more natural desire to justify oneself, should be subordinated to the importance of communicating only what is genuinely needed by the public, as opposed to keeping journalists' appetites whetted.

The satisfaction of having your say must be weighed against the likelihood of extending the negative coverage. You should remember that in the establishment of a poor image, the intensity of the negative coverage is not as important as its duration.

Frequently, the duration of bad publicity is increased by the desire of the well-meaning or self-righteous person at the focal point of a controversy to exercise their right to speak. What you don't say can't hurt you; whenever someone complains that what they have said is misinterpreted or taken out of context, the problem is often that they said anything at all. It's bloody difficult to take a silence out of context.

One of the responses which puts my teeth on edge is "No comment". You have sixteen journalists, eight of them wielding microphones and backed by camera operators, all clustered around the open door. The Subject comes out of the open door and heads towards his car.

"Mr Bloggs, could you tell us why—"

"Mr Bloggs, can you state why—"

"Can we have a comment, Mr. Bloggs, on—"

"What's the situation at the moment regarding—"

Instead of civilly shaking his head and keeping on the move towards his car door, the Subject stops, freezes his face, and says "No comment". Or worse "I have no comment to make this time." Immediately, any journalist with a tither of wit or persistence calls out:

"Mr Bloggs, why no comment, given that—"

"Your opponent said this morning, Mr. Bloggs—"

"When can we expect—"

A really good journalist will get a statement out there which establishes the story on tape:

"Your house burned to the ground today, two hours after you insured it for six million pounds, and this is the third time this has happened. Were you surprised by the happening?"

One way or the other, the subject's "No Comment" comment has made the footage much more interesting—and much less useful to him.

- If you have something to say, say it.
- If you have nothing to say, shut up.

  and
- Once you have said what you wanted to say, shut up.

The latter is a major problem for many people who are desirous of creating a good image for themselves. They cannot serve the coffee black. They make with the whipped cream until the end result sickens. Publisher Michael Korda put his finger on the matter.

"It is important to remember," he pointed out, "that a journalist's job is to *get* a story. He or she cannot ignore what you have said as if you never said it. There are complex rules, but in general, if you know something you don't want to see in the newspapers, don't talk about it."

Every public relations professional has a story to tell of some client who ignored this basic rule. My own favourite is a woman who rang me having already failed to excite her lawyer into sueing the newspaper which, that morning, had carried lengthy damaging quotations. Would I read the report and ring her back? I would. The newspaper was found on the desk of the lunchtime crossword addict, and I located the report. It was, as my caller had indicated, filled with damaging quotations. The only problem was that the quotations were all attributed to her. I rang her back. Had she said all of that stuff? Yes, she had. I sat in fuddled silence. But the reason she had said it, she quickly explained, was that the journalist had really put her under pressure.

What kind of pressure?

Well, he had been really very nice and he had said he appreciated he was invading her privacy, but this was an important story, and if she didn't give him the facts he might end up with something inaccurate, and she wouldn't want that, now, would she? She had given her all, and he had taken it down in expert shorthand and got it accurate to the last comma.

I began to understand the lethargy of this woman's lawyer.

Ah, she said, with the air of one delivering the clincher, but she had rung him back once she had had a chance to think about it, and asked him not to quote her. Asked him very definitely, she said. But he had pointed out that he had all of what she said taken down accurately and the piece had gone to the typesetters and there really wasn't anything he could do about it at that stage. So it had run. What had I to say about that? The only thing I could say was that when someone shoots the feet out from under themelves, it should not come as a shock to them to find that they don't have a leg to stand on, nor can they, with much credibility, blame someone else for their footlessness.

Sometimes, the sheer excitement of being in the eye of a storm, added to half-understood notions of how reporters operate, creates a lethally naive sense of control which is sadly rubbished as soon as the following morning's newspapers hit the street.

Above all, when you deal with journalists, tell the truth.

Unless in court, you don't have to swear to tell the whole truth, because if you always set out to tell every journalist the whole truth about everything, you will a) bore them to screaming point, and b) drop yourself in multifarious puddles.

If you are in a dodgy or a legally threatening situation, a good rule to remember is to answer the question you are asked, and *only* the question you are asked. (See next chapter for simple survival rules on radio and television.) Telling the truth has a number of advantages, apart from the important ethics of the thing. If you tell the truth, then you do not have to remember a lie, or confect phony details.

Detectives most frequently catch criminals, not because the criminals are guilty, but because they knit themselves a lie that unravels.

Journalists are at least as good as detectives at spotting—often unconsciously—the body language and the smell of fear which characterise someone flogging a fallacy as unvarnished verity. I have spent twenty years preparing businesspeople, clergy and politicians for current affairs TV programmes, and it never fails to astonish me how easy it is to spot when fancy footwork is going on. Having identified a lie, and wrung an admission from the speaker, it usually then emerges that telling the truth is a lot easier for that

TALKING TO REPORTERS: A GLOSSARY

■ Negotiate ground rules with reporters before you volunteer information. Knowing these definitions will help.

■ **Off the record** material may not be published or boradcast, period. Don't go off the record casually or with any one you don't have reason to trust.

■ **Not for attribution** information may be published, but without revealing the identity of the source. Always specify whether that applies to your company as well as you. Nail down the attribution the reporter will use—"a member of Acme Corp's two-man executive committee" vs. "an industry expert"—before you open your mouth.

■ **Background** usually means not for attribution, but don't take that for granted. Discuss it with the reporter.

■ **Deep background** usually means off the record. Again, make sure.

■ **Just between us** and other ambiguous phrases mean little to reporters. Don't use them.

■ **Check it with me before you use it** means just what it says. Specify whether the restriction applies to quotations as well as facts. When the reporter checks back, you have the right to correct errors and misunderstandings, but not to withdraw statements you now regret.

■ **Read it to me before you use it** gives you no right even to correct errors. All you get is advance warning of what the reporter will use.

■ **No** means that you have decided not to answer a reporter's question. Used judiciously, this is a lifesaver.

Fortune Magazine, June 1989

speaker than trying to play on a non-existent playing field.

In a difficult situation, do not seek to modify before you state the truth. If you are announcing an epidemic that has killed forty people, journalists do not want to be told about all the people who have so far escaped being infected, or about the effort that went into saving the lives of those who did not survive. Just announce the truth.

Which is not to say that, in a situation short of human tragedy, the truth cannot be presented with humour or with an angle. One of the best exampls of both happened when Ronald Reagan was demonstrating signs of age in the run up to the Presidential Election, and Walter Mondale was making it his business to ram home to the electorate that they just might be putting into the Oval Office a man considerably past his or anybody else's best.

So, at the next media pit stop on his nationwide tour, Mr Reagan commented that he knew a lot of people were thinking about the matter of age. Pause. But he was not going to make capital out of the youth and the inexperience of his opponent. Laughter from assembled multitudes, end of problem, on to the next town.

12

Live from Studio X —Coping with Bad News on the "Hot" Media

THE bad news has broken. They want to interview you for that night's TV news. Or they would like to have you in studio for that evening's tough current affairs programme. Or you know damn well they are going to be outside the door when you make a move to go home. Now is the time to deliver Hemingway's "grace under pressure", and survive, with style, in front of the cameras.

Your first option is not to be available. If you cannot contribute anything useful, then you should not go on the programme. A current affairs programme may be structured around you, with filmed inserts leading up to your planned appearance, and the production team will wish you in hell if you do not appear. However, them wishing you in hell for non-appearance may be marginally preferable to them *delivering* you to Hell, COD, which they can do if you agree to appear and thereby do yourself damage. Remember that the presenters cannot speculate on air about your non-appearance. They are entitled to say that they asked you and that you refused to appear, but no more than that. It is not the best publicity you could get, but on the other hand, it takes less than ten seconds to say, whereas your making a dog's breakfast over a riveting ten minutes of airtime may be as damaging as a liquidiser on the loose.

Not going on paid off handsomely.in the case of one recent high-profile TV programme. One side of a controversy was owned by what we'll call the Wilting Violet Company. This company's intentions were seen as threatening to the life, limb, morals, morale and personal happiness of everybody within a range of a hundred miles. The producer of the programme lined up fulminating community leaders, rampant politicians, innocent but inflamed bystanders, and a great deal of eye-catching, fear-inducing footage.

An invitation to participate in a programme was then issued to the Wilting Violet Company, which went away and fainted in coils. After sundry to-ings and fro-ings, the Wilting Violet Company decided to stay wilted, not to mention silent as the grave. The presenter duly appeared on the live programme, and said bitterly that the Wilting Violets didn't seem as enthusiastic as might have been expected to put their side of the story, but that he would play advocate for them. In other words, he would, out of decency and a desire to achieve that wonderfully mythological television ideal, "balance", present the line the Wilting Violets might be assumed to wish to be presented.

I have no doubt that the Wilting Violets sat and trembled while the programme proceeded. Violent, those trembles must have been at the beginning, but steadily diminishing as time passed, and as it became obvious that the fairminded, if less than happy, presenter was doing a better job of putting their side of the story than they might have hoped to do on their own behalf.

If you decide to be available, get your act together, and get all the information you are likely to need. There is a mile of difference between the way you will prepare for a TV news bulletin and the way you will prepare for a major TV current affairs programme lasting twenty minutes.

Time is of the essence. The TV news bulletin, if the item is very important and if it's not a strong news day, may see you speaking for as much as 40 seconds. Don't bank on it, though. The average "sound bite" going into American TV news bulletins at time of writing is 11 seconds. In the event that you cannot compress your story into that space, then you may find yourself and your item on the cutting-room floor. Before you go in front of a camera, whether in a studio or out of doors, work out what you want to say and what you don't want to say.

While you may not be able to control the questions asked of you, you will be able to control what you offer. In helping to achieve this, it may be worthwhile to purchase *Just a Few Words*, a paperback by one Terry Prone, which gives precise guidelines on how to survive various media interviews.

Alternatively, it may be desirable to rehearse with a competent coach. If you take professional advice and undertake a videotaped coaching session, keep it to yourself. TV journalists love "naturals". When they discover that a "natural" is actually an interviewee who takes public appearances seriously and prepares accordingly, they get notions that some Pygmalion somewhere is carving the interviewee out of raw soap and putting the words in his or her mouth. They hate to think that the subjects of their searing interrogation are prepared for any of the sear, preferring a kind of television journalism hare coursing, where the odds are on the side of the pursuer. If the subject gets torn apart while we watch, this is regrettable and was never intended, but shucks, isn't it great viewing?

Assuming that a current affairs programme is eager to have your body, mind and responses made available to viewers because of a bad news story, then you must first of all decide whether or not you wish to face up to the risks involved.

Given the option, go for a live broadcast, rather than a pre-recorded one. Novice TV performers always assume that they will do better if they are pre-recorded, because "If I don't get it right, they'll do it again." Uh, uh. If *they* don't do it right, they'll do it again. If *you* don't do it right, they may be in an awful hurry, and tell you it's grand, don't worry about a thing.

So not only are you irrevocably committed to tape,

but the editing of that tape is in hands other than yours. Even without malign intent, the programme makers will chop your input up to suit their needs, selecting what you may believe is least important for inclusion, and excising what you may believe is vital. Sometimes, there is intent which comes as near as dammit to malign. The classic example was when General Westmoreland was interviewed at enormous length by an American TV interrogator, and only tiny, damaging sections of the tape were used in the programme eventually broadcast.

Westmoreland was vexed enough to sue. CBS, the network involved, felt that the interview had followed its own express standards, which say, *inter alia*, that:

> *Interviews which are not spontaneous and unrehearsed are prohibited. An interview is not spontaneous or unrehearsed if*
>
> - *the questions are submitted to the interviewee in advance (but the interview will be considered spontaneous and unrehearsed if the advance submission consists merely of an outline of the general areas from which specific questions will be drawn)*
>
>   *or*
> - *there is an agreement not to use a particular general area as a basis for specific question;*
>
>   *or*
> - *there is an agreement not to ask specific questions;*
>
>   *or*
> - *the film, tape or transcript of the interview is submitted to the interviewee for approval or for participation in the editing process.*

Another example was when a spokesman for a company—again American—was interviewed at such length that the resulting transcript lasted twenty-two pages. Of those twenty-two pages, only one and a half were broadcast—again, the negative bits. In this instance, the company made a point of releasing the entire transcript to other media, to underline what they perceived to be the poisoned selectivity of the programme makers.

Pre-recorded, you are in somebody else's hands, and so a general rule worth following is to be willing to take part, but whenever possible, do it live.

When programmes are pre-recorded, it is possible to have them shot in all sorts of pleasing locations, although a location which is pleasing to the programme makers is not necessarily pleasing to a programme participant. One client of mine refused to take part in a programme which involved him walking through a factory he had closed down, realising that the echoing emptiness would make an emotive point which was unanswerable in words.

If the programme is live, you must ask questions and then set yourself tasks.

Questions:

- How long is the item?
- Where in the programme does it happen?
- What comes before it? If what comes before it is a filmed introductory piece, then what sort of content is covered in that filmed piece?
- Who appears in it?
- Who is doing the interview?

- ◆ Who else is in studio at the time?
- ◆ Will there be live input from an audience or on the telephone?

You are entitled to ask to see the filmed introduction, but there is no guarantee that they will agree, nor is there any requirement that they should. You are not entitled to demand a list of questions, although it is certainly acceptable to ask for a list of areas which are to be covered by the interview, and even if they gave you a list of questions, it would be of no value to you, since it is the supplementary, asked in response to what you have already said, which will cut you off at the knees.

Your Tasks

- ■ To prepare in advance to offer interesting information to the programme and, indirectly, to the viewers, rather than set yourself up as an Aunt Sally.
- ■ To prepare "added value" so that what you have to say immediately attracts attention, wins understanding and creates the possibility of your being remembered.
- ■ To dress in a businesslike way and turn up on time, sober and ready to do a professional job.
- ■ To answer the questions you are asked honestly and without flannel—and to take any opportunity offered to do more than merely answer questions. You're not there as a verbal yo-yo, twiddling on the end of someone else's string.

- To do your thinking in advance of the programme time, so that you do not waste the viewers' time being reflective and perplexed. Do this in your own time, please.

Above all, you must not waste time being paranoid. If the interviewer is out to get you, concentrating on that possibility is not likely to improve your performance. The overwhelming likelihood, however, is that the interviewer is *not* out to get you; just out to face you with the important questions he or she believes the public want asked, and determined not to let you waffle your way around important matters.

Terror of interviewers is often rooted in a conviction that any probing questions they may ask are generated by personal malice. This is almost never the case. In the majority of cases, the questions asked are the questions which should be asked. In the majority of cases, the tone in which those questions are asked is one which lends an edge to the broadcast programme.

There are exceptions, of course. The more ostentatious of those exceptions tend to be found in the USA, Morton Downey being the most recent example. But before Downey created a reputation for abusive interviewing, a man named Alan Berg had created a reputation for himself on local radio as a broadcaster of sporadic uncontrolled belligerence whose outbursts brought the Federal Communications Commission bagloads of letters requesting that he be taken off the air.

"Freedom of speech, the FCC would point out while answering those requests, was not illegal in the United States," Berg's biographer, Stephen Singular, later wrote. "As long as the First Amendment was intact and Berg avoided using obscenities, there was little the federal government could do to satisfy their complaints. Berg was almost never profane, at least not in his use of language. Obscenity was more likely to come from angry callers to his show. KGMC, the first station he had worked for, couldn't afford a tape-delay machine, which creates a seven-second gap between what the caller says and when it is broadcast. The device prevents a number of illegal words from hitting the air. Early listeners to his show were occasionally treated to an incensed caller telling the host to do something unnatural with himself. Yet for every person who loathed Berg's program, there was another who was enthralled with it. In the late 1970's a contest was held in Denver to determine who was the most liked and who was the most disliked media personality in town. Berg won both awards." (Stephen Singular, *Talked to Death. The Life and Murder of Alan Berg.* Beech Tree Books,William Morrow, New York, 1987)

To his listeners, Berg was either an agreeable stimulus or a maddening irritant. To an interviewee, even one as self-possessed as Rita Mae Brown, author of *Rubyfruit Jungle*, he was a much greater problem.

"I got thrown out by him," she told me. "He was a terribly neurotic and really a sick man, and I didn't say what he wanted me to say. I wasn't arguing with him. He was just off on some track—I don't know where—

and I just kept trying to talk in reasonable tones and he kept yelling and yelling and he finally said 'Get out of here, I can't interview you.'

So I left."

Maeve Binchy, on the other hand, has found interviews difficult, not because the interviewer was neurotic or sick, but because the interviewer had not had a chance to read the book about which he was to interview her, and in some cases, wasn't dead sure who she was.

"In Birmingham once, a young man said to me, just as we were about to go on the air, 'have you always been making your own furniture?'" Maeve recalls. "I thought about it and I thought I couldn't have climbed all these stairs to talk about making my own furniture. And I said, 'No, I've actually never made any furniture.' 'Oh, you're the *other* one,' he said. 'You're the one who wrote the big book!' That's the level very often."

The bottom line is that whether an interviewer is hostile, charming, informed, ignorant, intelligent or thick as two planks, your success or failure in the interview will be at least 80% due to your own competence or lack of it. If you are starting from a negative because the story about you, your organisation or your company is negative to start with, then there is a cloud and there is a silver lining. The cloud is best summed up by the American PR people, who hold that "if you're explaining, you're losing"; in other words, once you are trying to justify yourself, it is assumed that you are in the dock, and for good and sufficient reason. It takes a lot of content and charisma to get out of that position.

The silver lining is that bad news or hostile interviewing does attract viewer attention. So if you *do* produce content and charisma, the viewers will get a load of both.

13

Getting Away from Television: The Other Essential Points of Contact

WHETHER you are selling an idea, a personality, a political party, a fundraising effort, a product or a company, getting column inches or mentions on a radio or TV programme is only the beginning. You must never forget that you touch on your various publics in all sorts of ways, other than through media. You have all sorts of other interfaces with the people it is important that you reach. There are all sorts of contact points to which attention must be paid if you are marketing something, even if that something is just your wonderful self.

The following round-up is not comprehensive. Having taken a quick canter through it, you will quickly identify other contact points specific to your business or your key publics.

Having identified them, your next task is to make sure they are maintained as good conduits of your message; waffle- and rust-free.

Personal Contact

Once upon a time, I was directing a party political broadcast which homed in on one particular candidate. He was new to the game, and so his party wanted him minded, polished and presented in all of his facets to the eager public. He seemed to me as multi-faceted as a plate, but my cameraman was a creative genius and came up with pictures which, mated with evocative music, turned our political friend into a briefly impressive persona. Decision makers from the political party examined the end result and were euphoric. If I had the brains I was born with, I would have done some absorption of the euphoria, taken the money and shut up. Instead, I said that although it was a good programme, the actual product, out meeting people in the street, was lethal. What did I mean, lethal, they asked? Lethal as in kill you stone dead if you happened to be introduced to him, I said. Lethal as in offend you, bore you, de-motivate you, depress you and confirm you in your intention of exercising your franchise if only for the fleeting pleasure of doing him down at the ballot box. Lethal as in cyanide, I said.

Did I mean voters wouldn't find him an attractive personality?

I drew breath yet again, and made it as clear as I could that this man, at every point where he came in contact with real live voters, rubbed them the wrong way. He presented a hand to be shaken rather than with intent to shake. It fell into other people's grasp like a three-day-old plaice with mange of the gills. He looked over the shoulder of the person he was talking to in case he might miss someone more interesting.

He referred everything back to himself. In convers-ation, if you mentioned that you had a cold, he had a worse one. If you had a poodle with chilblains, he had a Great Dane with gangrene. If you had dry rot in your garage, his sittingroom was in the process of a meltdown to Australia. He walked in front of his canvassers like the Queen walks in front of Prince Philip, the vital difference being that Prince Philip is paid enough to make it worth his while to walk behind. His aftershave was so potent that if you stood near him, your fingernails turned blue from lack of oxygen.

When I finally ground to a halt, one of the party people responded, plaintively, that PR people didn't usually say things like that. He didn't actually voice what he was thinking, which was that PR was about gilding the lily and why didn't I just do it. If he had, I'd have told him that this was no lily, this was ragwort. You don't gild ragwort. You extirpate it.

Fair dues to the people involved, they did a fast

extirpation job on a lot of your man's worst habits, so that he stopped being a peripatetic plague and scraped home. Moral? No matter what publicity you get, if your job actually involves you in meeting people, then your performance at that meeting point had better measure up to your publicity or you will be rightly seen as not just inadequate, but phony, to boot.

Exteriors

How you look is your business. I do not subscribe to the "Dress for Success" school of thought, and am personally given to bleached hair, neon colours and tarts' shoes. However, the reality is that when your clothes, your weight, your halitosis or your speech patterns get in the way of the image you are trying to convey, it is worth scrutinising these things.

A caveat, before I get down to specifics. Thirty years ago, a university professor told a post-graduate student that this student should find himself some hidden job to do which did not involve talking to or with people, the reason being that the student had a pronounced rural accent, a tendency to put the "th" at the end of the word "throat" rather than the beginning, and could never pronounce the word "hundred" correctly—his version of the word was "hunthdert." The student grew up to be a radio and television presenter and a communications lecturer. He still can't pronounce "hundred" and I have the good fortune to be married to him. So yah boo sucks.

Not everybody has that innate self-confidence or the justification for it. Some people need to pay attention to their exteriors (personal and corporate) in order that those exteriors should not distract from the core of what they need to communicate.

Bobby is one of the brightest people I know. In his early twenties, he got into a business and started up the ladder at such speed that every time I talked to him he had a new and improved title. At twenty-eight, he was manager of his section, and in trouble. He was in trouble because his Managing Director, having promoted him in the expectation that the promotion would instantly result in the growth of personal *gravitas*, now felt that Bobby was not impressive enough. The Managing Director walked around the subject a lot, talking about prestige and status and stature, and Bobby got more and more terrified and confused. Eventually, a friend sat him down.

"OK, Bobby," said the pal. "You not up to the job?"

Bobby looked startled and made with the profanities.

"OK," the pal said. "You're up to the job."

Effing sure he was up to the job, Bobby said.

"Well, for starters, clean up the language," the pal said.

"Oh, come *on*, fer Chrissakes," Bobby began.

"One of the things that held Lee Iaccocca back in Fords was that he was always swearing in places where the rest of them weren't swearing," the pal said. Small silence.

"Does your MD swear at meetings?"

Bobby's head shook from side to side.

"No? Does your MD swear on the phone? At his secretary? OK—follow his example. Swear on your own time, at your own dog."

Bobby did a little practice under his breath.

"Tell you something else," the friend said. "You dress for the job you were doing five years ago."

"What's wrong with the way I dress?"

"Cheap. Crumpled. Trousers too long, hanging in bundles over your shoes. Nasty shoes. Not taken care of."

At this point, Bobby said the hell with it, he was the best man for the job and what had bloody suits and shoes got to do with it?

"Your MD is obviously not noticing how good you are at your job, because he can't see past the clothes you wear," the pal stated, scribbling on a sheet of paper.

When the pal handed over the sheet of paper, it bore the name of a high-class tailoring company in the city. Bobby, reading it, observed that this was the company that dressed one of the highest-profile TV comperes.

"Yeah," the pal said. "And remember, that particular TV guy is seen as a class act, not just a good looking fella in front of a microphone. *His* suits add to his general image and do not take from it."

"Cost me arms and legs to get a suit from them," Bobby said bitterly.

"Arms, legs and torso," said the pal. "Because it ain't gonna be one suit, it's gonna be three. And shirts. And silk ties. And classy shoes, and the cleaning and polishing to maintain all of these."

Bobby was silent, presumably giving thought to a second mortgage on his house.

"Now, we've got to look at the personal bit," the pal continued relentlessly.

Forgetting that he wasn't allowed to swear, Bobby told his pal to get his interfering hands, metaphorical though they might be, off Bobby's underwear.

"Not personal in that sense," said the friend. "Personal in the speech sense. Dis, Dat, Dese and Dose. Your dentals, my old pal. Words beginning with TH.

You pronounce them hard. Your whole family pronounces them hard. It does not matter that the rest of your family pronounce them hard, but if you are trying to impress your MD, dis is not de way dat you will get dere, you know?"

Bobby gritted his dentals, took speech lessons, and rehearsed a lot in the bathroom.

"THis toothbrush," he would say discursively, "is, THerefore, a THoroughly terrific THing."

When he got the new suits and the new dentals, it struck him he might have the hair styled differently. The end result crept up on the Managing Director, who could never quite put his hand on the moment his anxiety level began to drop, but drop it did.

Bobby and his pal still think all of this stuff about peripherals is daft. But if you're selling something, they reason, you start with the customer, and Bobby's customer is his MD.

Exteriors, by the way, are not confined to your personal clothing or speech. Have a look at how your premises looks.

Does it market you and your services properly, or is it a let down? For several years now, my own business has been fighting the good fight with an individual graffiti artist or—who knows?—a generation of graffiti artists. Some bad-minded activist wielding a spray-can decorates our gable end every weekend with assertions of perverse habits attributable to local worthies, with wild claims of sexual performance attributable to himself, and with speculations as to the physical endowment beneath their clothing of various females designated by initials. So, every Monday, one of our staff goes out with our corporate spray can and eliminates the weekend message.

Stand well back from your business and look at it as if you were a stranger, arriving for the first time:

- Location

  (Easy to get at? Do you need a map to send to people?)

- Exterior

  (Weeds in pathway? Potholes? Paint on exterior?)

- Interior

  (Paint? Air conditioning?)

- Uniform

  (Necessary to avoid confusion between customers and staff?)

- Livery

  (Should your vehicles carry your logo?)

- Crockery

  (Civilised china for guest cups of coffee/tea)

- Loos

  (Clean? Well-appointed?)

Oyez! Oyez!

Avast, me hearties! Listen to this blast of personal communication from someone dressed in eighteenth century town crier's gear.

Physical representation can be a very good meeting point between you and your customers. Remember the sellers carrying plates of cut-up Mrs Field's cookies and offering them as taste samples? Your representative can be in ordinary clothes, or in character uniform.

McDonald's, the hamburger people, do this idea proud, with their clown named Ronald MacDonald. To be selected as fit to wear the Ronald MacDonald uniform almost requires you to prove that your great-grandparents lived lives of untarnished rectitude. There are lengthy auditions. If selected, you go through a rigorous training procedure, which ensures that no matter what happens, you have an agreed corporate game plan to fall back on. It also ensures that your wig, make up and costume vary by not a millimetre from the next Ronald MacDonald uniform. Creativity you are not allowed to have. Uniformity rules, OK. When you make an appearance on behalf of MacDonalds, you are surrounded by unobtrusive minders, one of them equipped with a breath spray.

This minder hauls you off every twenty minutes or so and quickly squirts the breath freshener into your mouth, lest you pong the kiddies out of it. A blot on your uniform, an undeleted expletive or a tilt to your wig, and your make-up box and uniform are re-possessed and you are flung into outer darkness. All of which makes a lot of sense; clowning is a serious business, and any picturesque public representation of a business or organisation should be maintained to pristine standards.

Letters to the Paper

I have an old freelance journalist's loathing of letters to the paper. Or to any other medium, for that matter. If you are a freelance journalist, hungry for money and work (preferably in that order) you hate like hell people who are prepared to offer a newspaper column inches for free. If you write scripts for radio programmes, you have equally mixed feelings about listeners who provide, without charging, beautifully crafted minutes of monologue for the presenter of the show.

For the most part, if you are taking the initiative in seeking publicity, you should think in terms of placing stories or, if that fails, writing the story yourself. Letters come way down the line. On the other hand, there is one area where letters are the best of the available options. That is where a newspaper has been inaccurate or biased in reporting something in which you are involved. When that happens, you can get in touch with the newspaper's duty editor, explain your problem, and, if you explain it right, and it genuinely is a mistake or a mis-judgement on the part of the paper, the duty editor will make sure that a correction goes in the little correction box. But it will be the shortest correction humanly possible, and it will be in bed with three or

Poisons

Sir—On October 9 your newspaper ran a headline "chemists rapped on 700 child poisonings".

At no stage in my conversation with your reporter did I "rap" pharmacists. The responsibility for accidental child poisonings, which account for about 3,000 incidents and 1,000 hospital admissions annually, lies at many doors.

Doctors need to ensure proper prescribing, pharmacists need to ensure proper dispensing and, above all, parents need to ensure safe storage.

The unchanging incidence of child poisoning has led me to believe that parental and public education has failed. The secret of success in accident prevention is access prevention. Child resistant containers could prevent 60-70 per cent of serious poisonings, and only pharmacists can ensure their introduction for prescription medicines.

Eye-catching headlines such as yours distort facts, and only serve to distance professions which should be working together. I hope that pharmacists will accept my apologies and co-operate in reducing poisonings which are so distressing to small children.

DENIS G. GILL,
The Children's Hospital,
Temple Street,
Dublin 1.

four other corrections, some of which, either by virtue of the fact that their subject matter is quite different, or because the scale of the original insult is diametrically at variance with the scale of the insult done to you, will make your correction look damn silly.

In that instance, it is much better to write a good letter to the paper. The example on the page opposite shows a letter writer solving the problem the newspaper caused him with elegant precision. He does not launch into criticisms, first of all. He merely tells the story of the offence briefly and in quotes. Nine letter writers out of ten begin with a waffly whinge about the morals or intent of the writer of piece which irritated them.

"Dear Sir," they whimper. "Never have I been so gratuitously misquoted as I was in your recent execrable feature on the lifestyle of the sarcoptic mange mite, on which I would modestly claim to be the world's great expert..." By the time the reader has got to the end of the first sentence, he or she is confused. Not only that, but the urge to read further is beginning to recede somewhat. Professor Gill's letter instead nails the suggestion, implicit in the headline referred to, that he had said something which he now makes clear he didn't say. Thereafter, he goes on to make a substantive point. In the last paragraph he delivers a brisk kick to the newspaper and a generous and unwarranted apology to people who might have been offended by the original report.

Computer Networks

This is a small interface, but if you are in the financial services area or related business, or you want to reach people who are in that area, it may be worth considering. Increasingly, companies are tapping into

computer networks which give them information on screen about what has happened to the Dow Jones or in the Tokyo stock market that morning. These networks sometimes carry advertising or public relations information. It's worth exploring.

The Telephone

Yes, you can sell your story to a newspaper on the telephone. Or you can ring a radio programme which has an open phone line. Indubitably the most important function of the phone, however, is in conveying to potential buyers of your product or service how highly professional, warm and wonderful your operation is.

In order to convey that impression, your operation needs to come across on the telephone as warm, wonderful and professional. That means that every phone call should be answered within five rings. It should be answered with a clear description of who you are: "Good afternoon. This is the Frycicle company. Can I help you?" If a machine answers your phone, the voice should be your own, if you're a one-man or one woman-operation. I have a pal who bought a syndicated answering service voice, which, in transatlantic tones, used to promise in treacly tones that the owner of the phone would get right back to the caller. The caller, floored by the transatlantic voice, would be attacked by sudden doubts as to whether or not he/she had rung the wrong number, and the beep which was to cue him/her to speak, would instead leave him/her speechless.

If you use an answering machine, make sure that you check your messages every time you come into the house, and that you return them.

Market Research

Market research can be extraordinarily useful in generating publicity. Newspapers love studies which reveal that 43% of people have reservations about hitting their boiled egg on the sharp end, and that 29% of people would rather lose a tooth than an ear, or that a growing number of people are using sweeteners in their coffee. Must of what ends up in our newspapers arising out of market or attitudinal research has novelty value rather than real news value, but if you have commissioned the research, and if, as a result, you figure in the headlines, you may not care much about the semantics of the exercise.

Market research companies frequently run vast surveys with little addenda questions piggy-backing on the main questionnaire. These little piggy-back questions are like bucket-shop tickets on big airlines; the price is much more reasonable than if you want a cross section of the nation surveyed for an hour per individual. If you can think of some aspect of your business which, if researched, might turn up some odd facts, figures or trends, then that research could be useful to your marketing or publicity thrust or to both.

One food company recently came up with precisely this kind of idea. It surveyed mothers of very young

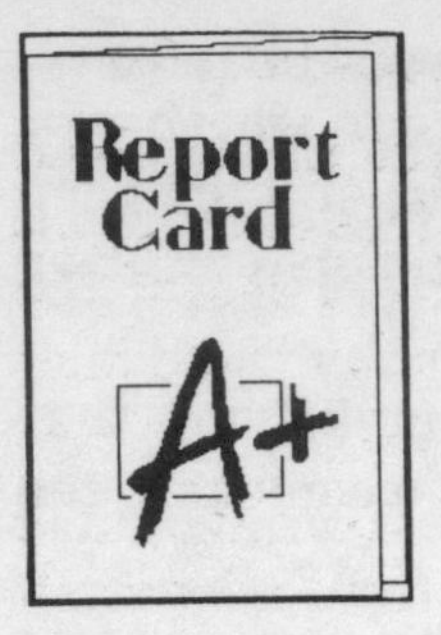

schoolgoers, asking them to specify what they put in their children's lunch boxes. The results of this survey may not have been very significant but the time of their release—the end of Silly Season and the beginning of the new school terms—was conducive to the achievement of considerable and positive coverage.

Writing Things

Newspapers, magazines and local radio stations swallow up great volumes of the written word. Each newspaper has its own staff, as does each magazine and broadcasting organisation. But they all have spaces for contributions from freelances or from people who have a special area of expertise. If you can cast yourself in that role, and if you can write about the area you know best in a lively interesting way, there is every chance that a newspaper will carry your feature. If it does, then hey presto, you have instant publicity. But you may have more than that.

Let's say you have recently bred a cross between a banana and a tomato. It tastes great and, sliced longways, is dead easy for sandwich-making. You have already had a launch of your cross-bred wonder and have achieved a certain level of publicity. However, you now wish to sustain your level of awareness. So you write a feature for a national newspaper on plant genetics and its risks. This feature does not give you any overt "plugs". It may mention your banato, but the key value for you is that the introductory paragraph will credit you with having created or generated the new food. It will re-cycle the story to your benefit.

A few weeks afterwards, you might think about sending to the provincial newspapers, free of charge, a few recipes to exploit the unique properties of the banato, and incorporating a photograph of the dishes resulting from these recipes.

At the same time, you could write a feature about the particular problems of marketing a brand new fruit/vegetable, and send it to a marketing publication, a feature about packaging a delicate ditto, and send it to a packaging magazine, and write an article about the tax problems facing entrepreneurs in the horticultural business, sending it to a monthly business magazine.

Public Meetings

There are people who leave their warm private houses in the evenings and go to community centres and local hotels to participate in meetings and seminars and to provide an audience for wandering lecturers. There are people who leave their own counties at weekends and travel across the country to attend conferences, AGMs and other gatherings which purport to improve their professional performance but which, it can be argued, often do very little other than temporarily improve their social life and give them the material for a better contacts book.

These people are reachable. They are collected together in one place, and if you can ensure that you are the lecturer who addresses them in that one place, you will have reached an audience that may be worth reaching. So research their meetings, and find out who is in charge of selecting the *dramatis personae* to fill the stage or stand behind the podium. You then do a selling job on yourself as a stunning speaker. (Make damn sure you are a stunning speaker. Take lessons if you need to.) When you have worked out a great speech filled with startling concepts, then give serious thought to issuing a press release which indicates that you articulated all of this stirring stuff at such a location on such a day—you never know, you might get some coverage for it.

14

Timing and Thank-Yous —and Final Tips

Good timing is vital, in publicity terms. Being the first to do something can be helpful, as long as the thing you're doing is interesting to people at that time. There have been a great many scientific discoveries and other developments which were disregarded by the public of the time, but taken to the heart of later generations.

If you *are* the first with a piece of news, make the most of it. By shutting up. It may sound like a contradiction, but many a great publicity campaign has imploded because someone talked too much too soon. A good secret, spread among too many people, gets to a journalist. What may result is one story instead of a blitz of publicity. So if you are operating a small company, or planning a controversial political campaign, tell the details to as few people as possible, and make those people aware that careless talk costs headlines.

Timing also depends on informed opportunism. Of course, we must all have core values, corporate direction, strategic plans for the next five years, career paths mapped out well in advance, but none of that worthy map-making should distract us from making the most of an opportunity if it arrives in front of us with OPPORTUNITY printed across its tee shirt.

The story of just such an opportunity has been told by Robert J. Wood, an American who has been in the PR business for almost half a century, and whose client, Hallmark Cards, was centre stage.

"Hallmark started to build a warehouse and distribution center in New Jersey," says Wood. "The steel skeleton was just about complete when somebody discovered that a pair of birds had built a nest in a corner. There were eggs in the nest.

"Hallmark ordered all construction stopped immediately. It stayed stopped until the birds finished raising their family and flew away.

"The story had an appropriately happy and sentimental ending. After the birds had departed and just before construction resumed, a hurricane blasted through the area.

"If the building's walls and roof had been partially installed at the time, there would probably have been heavy damage. As it was, the steel skeleton presented no face to the winds, and there was no damage at all.

"Kindness had been rewarded!"

This story charmed a journalist named Max Gunther when he heard of it—which coincided with his researches for a feature on the "love industry". In the course of his researches, he had been asking questions of Hallmark. The birds' nest saga featured in his final report, much to the delight of Hallmark and its PR advisers. (Robert J Wood with Max Gunther, *Confessions of a PR Man,* New American Library)

If an opportunity presents itself, grab it. But grab it only after you have thought about it. Many a man has been so maddened by what another has said about him that he has determined to ram the words publicly down the other's throat, only to find that, because of inadequate preparation, his forearm gets bitten off down to the elbow. Before you involve yourself in public controversy, stop and think. But stop and think quickly. I once had a call from a man who came to see me with a dossier which he wanted to discuss on a radio programme as a result of a four-minute interview with someone who had said hostile and inaccurate things about one of my visitor's products. Reading the material, I had to admit that the negatives expressed were not defensible in court, but, on the other hand, none of them were of earth-shattering importance, either. True, my visitor said, but he wanted them corrected. He wanted to go on the programme and answer all of these accusations. He had no interest in any other action, and so a fast phone call on his behalf to the programme involved seemed like a good idea.

"What day did this happen on?" I asked as the phonecall went through.

"Tuesday," he said, promptly.

"*Today's* Tuesday," I said.

"Tuesday the 5th," he said. I looked at the calendar, startled. It was now the twelfth.

"Last month," he finished. I cut off the phone call.

"Let's get this clear," I said. "This happened, what—six weeks ago?"

An affirmative nod.

"What have you been doing in the meantime?"

"Getting together the ammunition."

"For *six weeks*?"

"I do my research carefully," he said.

"This may be true and praiseworthy," I told him. "But there's not a chance that the programme will take a response from you now. A response is like a pendulum—you've got to hit it when it's still swinging. This pendulum stopped swinging weeks ago. If you want some kind of justice, then write to the producer, and you may, if you're very lucky, get a letter that approximates to an apology for the fact that they allowed a man to make criticisms of you on the air without giving you the chance to counterbalance what he said. But, frankly, don't hold your breath. If I were the producer, I would be asking why you hadn't asked for a chance to balance it nearer the time."

"I don't think that's fair," he said, and took his dossier and went away. I was sorry for him, but there is a tide in the affairs of men which, taken at the flood, leads on to fortune, and he'd missed it.

The importance of timing should never be

underestimated. Neither should the importance of saying "thank you". A journalist may find your story particularly attractive and make an extra effort to help readers to think so too. Or a journalist who does not find your story that attractive may, out of the goodness of his or her heart, do you a favour and dress up nothing to look like something. A third possibility is that a journalist may deliver your story with scrupulous accuracy. One way or the other, the journalist deserves a civil thank-you note. Journalists almost never get such notes from the people who should send them, although the flow of letters of complaint is fairly constant.

Civility, to journalists and other human beings, is greatly interfered with when people who are in the spotlight begin to believe their own publicity. If you're in the spotlight, don't. For starters, the world is full of millions of people who have not, or could not, or would not read what has appeared about you. Among those who have read it, the number who will recall anything of what was written is tiny, because we live in a century when we are constantly bombarded with data.

Newspaper readers scan. Television viewers watch. Radio listeners hear. All of them forget the bulk of what was briefly at the front of their minds, and unless you are startlingly memorable, you're likely to be part of what they fail to recall.

That should be viewed positively and negatively. Bad publicity passes as the sparks fly upwards. Today, there is a report in a newspaper which suggests that your company is not doing as well as it might, or that your arrival has not improved the performance of your dance troupe as much as had been expected. Tomorrow, they're on to somebody else, and only a handful of people remember what was written about you. The fact that every word of what was written is now etched in acid on your heart is beside the point. Do not overestimate the national impact of the story. Just identify what important or vulnerable groups or individuals have been reached by it, and make sure that their minds are put at rest. This is often better done by personal contact than by whimpering to the editor of the offending publication.

Never lose sight of the fact that reaching the general public is not half as effective as reaching the public that matters to you. If you are trying to reach illiterates to offer them lessons in reading, then you do not seek lengthy features in upmarket national newspapers. In print, all you ever want are two-sentence mentions in free local papers or popular magazines. But your main emphasis has to be on getting radio and television coverage, because the illiterate are oral culture people: radio and TV are where they get the bulk of their information.

Reaching an important audience may require more action than getting a feature published in a newspaper. Assuming that you achieve the publication of the all-time perfect feature, you can then ensure that all of your target audience reads it if you extract it and mail it to them. When a radio commentator of impregnable popularity said positive things about a clever gadget a friend of mine had invented, the friend got a transcript of the comment and posted it to every potential purchaser whose name occurred to him, and the payoff was handsome.

"It wasn't a bad payoff for one free gadget, a one page transcript and a few postage stamps," he told me later.

It is worth emphasising, however, that a free sample is not a bribe, unless you happen to make Lamborghini vehicles. Send somebody a Lamborghini as a free sample and it is not only excessive, it's crude. Be careful.

Be legal.

Above all, if you are setting out to achieve free publicity, as opposed to the kind you buy from an advertising agency, do not lose sight of your objective. You are not buying publicity, and so it should not cost you an inordinate amount. Keep detailed accounts of all expenditure incurred, whether in making phone calls, having pictures taken, FAXing things, buying display materials or taking a journalist for a drink, and present them to your accountant or directly to the income tax people.

One Final Word

Publicity is not hard to get. What is extremely hard to establish is a firmly based image which is sustainable and renewable over a period of time. That is a matter of planning, experience and finely-honed skill which is worth paying for.

But at what stage do you need to stop doing your own public relations and hand the task over to a professional consultancy?

I suggest that you need to do it when you find that image-management is getting in the way of your doing your main job. A pal of mine, who started a business and has seen it grow into a massive operation, put it slightly differently.

"One day, I realised that the company was paying someone to come in and put water in our plants, but I was managing the entire thing and at the same time, doing the publicity—badly. So I told my board what I thought we needed to spend, and once they had come out of shock, I asked for proposals from three of the best companies, and picked one of them."

If and when you get to a similar point, keep my company's name among the three you invite to tender.

Please!

Write and Get Paid for It

by

Terry Prone

If you enjoy writing and would like to make some money out of it, here is the book for you. Terry Prone explores all the markets, new and old.

Just A Few Words

by

Terry Prone

All you need to know about speaking in public

POOLBEG

The Secret Army
The IRA 1916-1979

by J. Bowyer Bell

The definitive work on the IRA. It provides an absorbing account of a movement which has had a profound effect on the shaping of the modern Irish state.

J. Bowyer Bell is a leading expert on terorism and unconventional war.

The Poolbeg Golden Treasury of Well Loved Poems

Edited by Sean McMahon

By the compiler of *Rich and Rare*

and

The Poolbeg Book of Children's Verse

A delightful anthology of everyone's favourite poems, from Shakespeare to Patrick Kavanagh

POOLBEG